BUILT IN
NEW ZEALAND

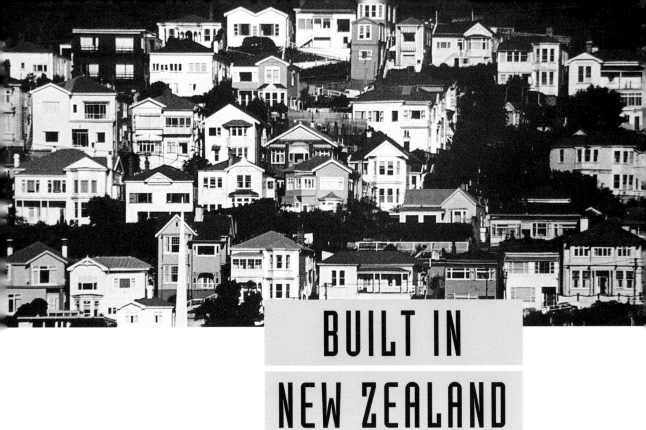

BUILT IN
NEW ZEALAND

The Houses
We Live In

William Toomath

HarperCollins*Publishers New Zealand*

For my grandsons — Andrew, Paul and David

Only connect . . .

E.M. Forster

Front cover: Villa entrance, Herne Bay, Auckland. By kind permission of
the owners, Ron and Laraine Farmer. (*Ralph Talmont*)
Title page: Houses on Mt Victoria hillside, Wellington, *c* 1960
Back cover: Houses on Mt Victoria hillside, Wellington, 1992

First published 1996
HarperCollins*Publishers (New Zealand) Limited*
P.O.Box 1, Auckland

Copyright © William Toomath 1996

ISBN 1 86950 219 1

Design and production by 2D Design Limited
Typesetting and artwork by HieroGraphics
Printed by HarperCollins, Hong Kong

Contents

Acknowledgements

This book's seed came from a talk given at the 1992 Conference of the Stout Research Centre, Victoria University of Wellington, concerning New Zealand's "bungalow years" between the two World Wars. From two years spent in the United States during the 1950s I had remained curious about similarities between the ordinary houses of that country and this, in particular from the Victorian age. I have to thank Professor Clarence Aasen for his nomination on that occasion (and his continual support thereafter), which led me to explore more fully the American influences on our everyday houses.

My thanks go to Paul Bradwell, publisher at HarperCollins Ltd in Auckland, for his invitation in 1993 to develop that conference paper (then published in the *Stout Centre Review*) towards a book; and subsequently to Mark Bathurst as senior editor, for encouraging me to broaden its scope and to seek the global origins of New Zealand's common houses. His skilful hand revealed the precision of the written word and his graceful diplomacy guided the work through its inevitable times of stress. I thank historian Ian Wards for his early encouragement and positive support; and I am indebted to Hugh Price for his wise guidance to a novice in the publishing world. To Lola Short, as my constant helper and tireless guide towards clarity, the book and I owe much. Michael Howard and David Price are thanked for computer aid at the crucial moment of my need for conversion. And a debt is owed to "providence" for guiding me so often to key information by pure chance.

I gratefully acknowledge the assistance of the literature programme of the Arts Council of New Zealand Toi Aotearoa (now Creative New Zealand), whose generous grant facilitated further research and full documentation.

I am grateful to David Gebhard, University of California, Santa Barbara, for seeing my mission as an "exciting project" and for his stimulating critique; and to Dr Abigail Van Slyck, University of Arizona, Tucson, for her encouragement and friendly interest. To many others I offer my thanks for their assistance with information, documents and discussion, including Mark Brack, Diann Cade, Chris Cochran, Tony Ellis, Robin Skinner and Reg Tye. And to the builders and owners, at home and abroad, of those countless houses freshly discovered and now regarded as familiar faces, I owe a great debt.

I thank the many friendly librarians and staff who gave assistance, both locally and overseas, at the Alexander Turnbull Library, Wellington (Barbara Brownlie in particular); The Athenaeum of Philadelphia (Bruce Laverty); Auckland Art Gallery (Roger Blackley); Auckland Museum Library (Gordon Maitland); The Bancroft Library, University of California, Berkeley (Richard Ogar); Los Angeles Public Library (Carolyn Cole); New York Public Library; Oakland Public Library, California (Bill Sturm); Otago Settlers Museum, Dunedin (Michael Findlay); RIBA Library, London; University of Auckland Architecture Library (Wendy Garvey); Victoria University of Wellington Library and Schools of Architecture and Design (David Kernohan, Gavin Woodward); and, especially, The Winterthur Library, Wilmington, Delaware (Neville Thompson and Pat Elliott) — the only research library I found that afforded 24-hour access!

By Their Buildings
Ye Shall Know Them

HIGH among the pleasures of foreign travel is the savouring of a culture different from our own. We interpret the differences from our familiar norm — or note surprising similarities — and drawing on these make assumptions about the local people's way of life. We observe the external signs and feel we have gained some intimate insight into the people's social character.

Above all, to walk among the houses in a foreign town is to capture the essence of its people's values, traditions and popular culture. Often, the older and more compact the town the clearer the impression gained. **1, 2** We "read" the houses, their grouping and their details, as products of a culture held in common — of which the houses are the public face. We are truly on others' home ground; and the feeling of its distinctive forms, **Pl. 1, Pl. 2** in comparison with our own, affects us strongly.

Doubtless, those other people visiting New Zealand would feel they gathered an impression of our national culture from similarly observing its distinctive public face – that of our common houses, and the pattern of life in our domestic streets. For ourselves, however, the features that would make our Kiwi houses distinctive in the eyes of others are blurred by familiarity in our own. Inevitably we take them for granted because they are our everyday background. We seldom see them acutely in the way that a visitor does. But if we can detach ourselves on our own home ground to look at and see our typical New Zealand houses with fresh eyes, as if we were in a foreign place, what might we learn about ourselves — about our values, traditions and social ways?

To do this we need to cancel the familiarity of our houses, to

Pl. 3, Pl. 4

1. (left) Urbania, near Urbino, Italy. A Latin sense of order and continuity is seen in these harmonious forms, arising from a shared response to local climate and materials. The church tower is the pivot of the community.

2. (right) Ohrid, Macedonia, in southern Yugoslavia. Western Asia and classical Europe meet in an overlay of Ottoman on Greek city life, showing signs of an erratic evolution.

See also **Pls. 1 - 4** *between pages 26 and 27.*

defamiliarise their appearance, and come upon them anew, as with the eyes of a stranger. We need to be able to discern their individuality, their New Zealandness, and to mark it for further enquiry; also to note their similarity to houses seen elsewhere. All our New Zealand houses are recent in world terms, and their origins lie beyond our shores. They have been born of successive waves of influence from abroad, impinging on the local necessities and material resources, and coloured by a growing sense of our own nationality.

From the first elegant Georgian-colonial houses, in a style brought here by the traders and missionaries of the 1820s and 30s, to the unsophisticated Californian bungalows of the 1920s, our commonest New Zealand houses have been our versions or reinterpretations of other countries' practices and fashions. Along the way we have turned them to our own choice, given them our own stamp, imprinted them with our own national characteristics. And now, in turn, these houses stand to be read like a book — a kind of serialised self-portrait of ourselves.

It is often stated that a nation's architecture provides a true picture of its culture at any particular time. My own version (with apologies to the Bible) is "By their buildings ye shall know them". And of all buildings, the common man's house is the staple fruit of every culture.

Built in New Zealand ventures a reading of our more common types of houses for the historical light they throw on the shaping of ourselves as New Zealanders. In order to bring into focus our main formative period, the book's scope extends from the 1800s to the start of the 1940s — from the time of the first settlers to the Second World War.

Older houses are helpful tools in the search for an understanding of cultural roots: they bear the expressive imprint of the character and aspirations of the society in which they were designed. In this book, many types of houses and building practices adopted or developed in New Zealand are identified and traced back to their sources. Comparison by visual evidence is used to clarify the path wherever possible, to establish links with precedents from overseas as well as to explore meanings underlying our house designs back through centuries. Not only does the British contribution emerge, as might be expected given our European background, but also the unexpectedly constant, if clandestine, liaison with our neighbour across the way — the United States.

The reasons behind these alignments or preferences are important, as they reflect our forebears' choice of the image to be projected as "home", itself an assertion of their self-esteem, of aspirations and emulations, as well as a statement of social position, roots, claims and celebrations. Our forefathers were conscious of making tentative beginnings in a new land, and moved towards a new spirit of freedom in their independent efforts. Their loyalties, as revealed in the popular choice of house designs — especially in those based on American models during a period of at least 50 years — often seem to be at strange variance with their professed sentiments for their British "home" in the "old country".

A penetrating look at familiar things can prompt new questionings, and can reveal unexpected answers when set against our common assumptions. As T.S. Eliot wrote:

We shall not cease from exploration
And the end of all our exploring
Will be to arrive where we started
And know the place for the first time.

Chapter 1

Homes People Make

Elemental forms

ALONG the shore at Kororareka in the Bay of Islands, in the late 1830s, stood a straggle of wooden houses whose shapes could have been matched on shores half the world away. New Zealand's pioneer European-type dwellings were not invented in a vacuum but had family among "folk" forms in many other countries. Elemental house shapes like these arise, with practical logic, out of man's creative use of available building materials to shape economical enclosures. They represent what people have been capable of building for themselves, from inherited knowledge and with little assistance from skilled builders.

Very common among these primitive and folk forms (in the Western

3. *Basic two-roomed cabins like this are universal, in every material. Built around earliest Auckland and 1860s gold-rush Arrowtown, just as here in Wellington's Tinakori Road.*

4

world at least) is the rectangular walled hut or cabin. A universal type for centuries, it usually has two rooms side by side (although sometimes only one) under a gabled roof with its ridge parallel to the longer wall. Examples are legion, from crofters' huts in the Orkneys to cottages in old Thorndon in Wellington. Generally speaking, the width of the plan form of this simple house is around 13 to 17 ft. (4 to 5 m), its length with two rooms being about 30 to 33 ft. (9 or 10 m).[1]

3

In late medieval English cottages the larger room, known as the hall, was a combined living room and kitchen including the hearth and entry door, with a sleeping "chamber" alongside and possibly a ladder into the roof space. An adequate dwelling, this rectangular hut form can be traced back to primitive origins, shortly after the dawn of civilisation. Up to about 9000 years ago (7000 BC), when constructing his dwellings man seems to have thought in terms of the rotation of a simple linear structural form around a central point, to form a private enclosure. Thus the rounded hut was the universal, and probably oldest, type of home after the cave. But there is evidence of rectangular houses in the very first towns known to history, built around 7000 BC in Anatolia (now Turkey) and Jericho in Palestine. Here it is evident that man's epochal steps towards a synthetic order, based on straight line and right angle, had led to the first rectangular dwellings. Built with thick walls of sun-dried bricks and flat roofs, apparently of baked mud over saplings, they were early expressions of man's taking control through a concept of quadrangular order.[2]

Pl. 5

From some 2000 years ago, evidence exists of the use of heavy timber frames for quadrangular huts and villas in the Roman occupations of northern Europe and Britain. After the Romans left Britain four centuries later, those timber techniques disappeared; but versions were reintroduced by Saxon and Norse invaders in subsequent centuries. From these was descended the much-loved English rectilinear cottage, reaching its prime between three and four centuries ago during the Elizabethan and Stuart reigns.[3]

Pl. 6

To this basic plan form, rooms could be added over time, either to the hall end or across the back of the cottage — commonly in the form of a lean-to, with the main roof continuing down or set to a lesser slope. In hotter climates, a porch or veranda could be added across the front, with a similar lean-to roof. The familiar profile of the folk-style rural cottage thus emerges, with its peaked gable ends flanked by lean-to roofs. We will encounter it in many variations throughout the tropics and into the temperate zones, from the West Indies to the American Midwest, and from the lower Mississippi to New Zealand.

On different scales, with and without lean-tos or verandas, the rectilinear cottage unit appears universally through recent centuries, in dwellings of single-storey, one-and-a-half or two-storeys height. Its simplest of living rooms has contained the essence of "home" in all cultures. With hearth and kitchen at one end, and dominated by a large, all-purpose table as the centre of family activities, such a room can best symbolise home life. The warmth of timeless peasant houses, and the feeling of homeliness imparted by the woman in her own domain as home-maker, are present

4

4. *Woman the indomitable home-maker. Preparations for a bushman's Christmas dinner, North Auckland, 1903 — defying reality with style.*

in this all-in-one living space. (Interestingly, we are reverting, in our servantless, latter-20th-century open-planning of houses, to the unified living space ideal after a century or two of splitting family activity into specialised cells — kitchen, dining room, drawing room, parlour, den and so on.)

Families of house forms

A direct way of expanding the basic long-and-narrow hut plan from the start was to double the unit into a squarer four-room layout, commonly known overseas as a double pile plan. But whereas gabled roof construction was usual for the longitudinal hut, with the ridge member supported on high gable wall peaks, a fully hipped roof on low walls was commonly adopted over this squarer plan. The four-square, hip-roofed cottage form is readily recognisable worldwide, from Georgian England to eastern Europe, and in every New Zealand town through our first 100 years and more.

At this point it may be helpful to clarify the terms *gabled* and *hip-roofed*, since they appear frequently through our story. For sloping roofs, in simplest terms:

> *gabled* houses have walls carried up to roof peaks;
> *hip-roofed* houses have horizontal eaves all round.

Gable ends are often ornamented, and the two forms may occur combined.

Families of elementary house forms — relatively innocent of conscious style, and conservative in structure — have been the basis of the common man's house through thousands of years.

The nature of building materials to hand also plays a leading role in shaping a house. Whereas the customary rectilinear sense of order guided the use of smaller units such as bricks, forest trees themselves implied straight walls and rectilinear houses. Equally, saplings and reeds were bundled and arched for strength, leading to vaulted rectangular house forms — used widely, from the first ancient Mesopotamian towns to certain pre-colonial Maori houses (as drawn by Polack in the 1830s). In other cultures, blocks of stone or dried earth — even of ice — were stacked to enclose space in a domical structure.[4]

5

Adding to the mix of folk forms in early New Zealand days were certain other features and elements, gathered from sources of colonial experience worldwide. Some originated from coping with uncomfortably hot climates in the tropics — verandas, louvred shutters and wide eaves. Some arose from an appreciation of the good life that such climates can engender — airy rooms with French doors and broad screened terraces. Others arose from constructional forms bringing together several of these features, creating notably the pyramidal roof sweeping out on all sides over sheltered verandas (see Chapter 5). Thus an international family of venerable house types, extended by the fruit of more recent colonial adventure, lies behind our early New Zealand house forms — probably accounting for some of the disconcerting likenesses to our own houses that we occasionally discover in foreign places.

6

5. *A Maori fishing village, probably at Poverty Bay, drawn in the 1830s by dynamic Jewish trader J.S. Polack. Houses were built with bundles of raupo reeds lashed together into structural forms.*

6. Eckford Homestead, built at Maraetai c 1850 (now at Howick Historical Village). This time-honoured and accomplished colonial house form is distributed across the world's subtropical zones.

Populist house forms

AT more advanced levels of house construction, the folk strain was carried into general "populist" houses through the work of skilled tradesman builders, erecting houses either to order or on speculation. The basic folk forms were still present but with improved handling of space, fittings and materials, as well as with greater ambition in their external design. A wider variety of house shapes resulted from reworkings of the traditional forms by builders, operating in a commercial environment. As a result, folk forms became overlaid by artifice and transient fashion: elements were modified and features added to meet social standards and aspirations. In time a more consciously sophisticated attitude to architectural style became part of the social demand. And since "style" meant status throughout the 19th century, and generally entailed enrichment by conspicuous decoration, ornament is a readily visible key to the changes made to house types through New Zealand history. The key of applied ornamentation is, indeed, frequently used in this book to unlock a fuller understanding of our home-building history.

Certain changes, however, sometimes occurred in the basic folk forms themselves. One such variation, emerging in the early 19th century, involved forming a break in the front face of the house by projecting one room forward a little, usually as a gabled wall. For the common man, a wish to escape plainness was met by modifying one of his two front rooms, thus locating the gable wall asymmetrically. As we shall see, this simple device has liberated the shape of common houses over the past two centuries. Familiar to us on our Victorian villas as the gabled bay to one side of the veranda, Americans know it by the descriptive term "upright and wing".[5]

Basic folk forms are recognisably similar in many countries, particu-

7. *The folk forms of rectangular hut, veranda and lean-to, built c 1860 and showing an awareness of Gothic styling in the dormer and veranda details. Windows are of pre-Victorian casement type.*

larly during pioneering phases and in rootless communities springing from events like gold rushes and colonial settlement. Their subsequent development into populist houses by knowledgeable builders, however, makes them individual as they acquire distinctive characteristics which reflect a **7** specific culture and time. They become elaborated by features deriving from details of architectural styles, or designers' innovations. These come not from an anonymous vernacular: they stem initially from the work of inventive architects or their equivalents, and are spread by built examples or by plan books promoting house designs. In the end, houses present the popular culture of their particular time and locale, and reveal little of the folk elements behind their form.

In later 19th-century New Zealand, such elaborations of the basic house included the adding of fretwork and moulded ornament on veranda posts and eaves, double-hung window bays, enriched wooden cornices and eaves brackets, ornate designs on gable ends — and much more (see Chapter 7).

It is intriguing that the nature and patterns of our most commonly added enrichments turn out to be closely similar to those used across the United States on their typical houses, and not similar to the equivalent design features applied to Victorian houses in Britain.

Chapter 2

New Zealand Beginnings

The Georgian spirit

THROUGH the latter three quarters of the 18th century — roughly the reigns of the first three Georges — the predominant interest driving architectural design in Britain was the classical spirit, ultimately inspired by Palladio's reworking and humanising of the formal grandeur of Imperial Rome.

Scaled down to a domestic level this spirit lay behind the quiet symmetries of the Georgian style. A central emphasis in the design was

8. *The Moot, Downton, Wiltshire, as remodelled in 1720. This early but exemplary English Georgian country house displays the style's most characteristic features.*

provided by entrance doorway and hall placed in the middle of the plan. Buildings and houses in this Georgian manner were conceived as if they were rectilinear solids hollowed out. Their structurally neutral walls were punctured at regular intervals by upright windows, while a calm horizontal format governed the design as a whole. Rather than seeking individual dramas, this disciplined architecture relied on proportions controlled by formula to achieve simple harmonies and an overall clarity. Roof forms were geometric prisms of moderate slopes, underlined by firmly horizontal eaves.

8

The apparent "normalcy" of such an undemonstrative style meant that it could be handled effectively by the unsophisticated and the provincial: lay designers and local builders could arrive at straightforward combinations of standard elements, sure of pleasant proportions. In rural versions it was close to a folk building manner, a vernacular based sensibly on essentials. It brought medieval irregularity under control. And it was not lacking in charm, nor opportunity for craftsmen's embellishments.

New Zealand's earliest European houses were built when this well-mannered discipline still held sway in Britain. In our frontier conditions from the 1820s, this modest style provided a workable and pleasant basis. We acquired practical rural traditions of building which, along with British nautical traditions, provided neat and tough building solutions.

The new colony of New South Wales

THE awakening of such developments in New Zealand must be sought in Australia, over 1900 km to the west across the Tasman Sea. The appointment by the British government in 1793 of an energetic and sharp 28-year-old, Samuel Marsden, to assist the hard-pressed chaplain of the new convict colony in New South Wales, was to set in train a sequence of events which would lead to the first European settlements in New Zealand. It was, interestingly, Britain's loss of her American colonies following the Revolution of 1776 that brought about the penal settlement of New South Wales in the first place. Founded on data from Cook's 1769 exploration, Sydney replaced the previously convenient colony of Virginia, to which, for 150 years, England's unwanted prison surplus had been transported.

Whereas the convicts transported to America could be sold at £20 per head as labourers to the established settlers, convicts to Australia could not easily be disposed of in the void of that country in 1788. In the six years prior to Marsden's arrival, a morally loose, military-directed community barely survived. Among their number, whether convicts, guards or ship's companies, skills had to be found to deal with their needs for shelter and sustenance. Slowly they were housed in barracks and huts, erected by the first carpenters in Australia.[1]

Huts and simple one-storey houses were built with bricks, clay being used riskily for mortar in the absence of lime; or with heavy timber framing, widely spaced in the age-old way and sometimes walled with cabbage-tree slabs set vertically. Often the spaces between framing were filled with brick panels protected outside by weatherboards split from hardwood logs — just as was done in Virginia 180 years earlier (see Chapter 4).

By the time of Marsden's arrival in 1794, the pattern of house building around Sydney Cove had a clear enough character: the general run was of single-storeyed rectangular houses covered by the simplest of hipped roofs sloping at 45 degrees with close-clipped eaves all round, on plain walls with regularly spaced openings. Brick chimney shafts stood proudly against external walls. Gable ends were only rarely seen on the occasional farm or storage building, where horizontal weatherboards also put in an appearance.[2]

These first rough antipodean builders tried to reproduce, against severe limitations, the vernacular cottage types which they knew at home, resembling in particular those of the counties around London, between Sussex and Essex. No verandas are yet in evidence, and no ornament. Neither climate nor ease has so far made its mark. A uniformity of roof shapes, of wall heights and of basic plans speaks of a military organisation – in contrast to New Zealand's first European town about 40 years later at Kororareka, with its haphazard multiplicity of building forms.

By the early 1800s, though, the first, rustic New South Wales houses had more sophisticated counterparts in the houses of the better-off on their farmlands at Parramatta. Two, in a Georgian manner, are of note: Samuel Marsden's two-storey, hip-roofed, plain rectangle, built by the colonial government in a rural weatherboard style familiar in Kent; and Lieutenant John McArthur's tallish, one-storey, hip-roofed, brick cottage with a stiff veranda across its front at Elizabeth Farm, dating from 1793.

9

Elizabeth Farm cottage with its front veranda of c 1795, one of the first in Australia (based on a drawing by J. Lycett, 1824).

9. *Reverend Samuel Marsden's cottage at Parramatta, Sydney, built c 1800: a colonial version of rural Georgian proportions and regularity (and with no veranda in this sketch of 1836).*

A colonial version of the Georgian style was clearly established in New South Wales at an early date.

Marsden makes a start

THE circumstances surrounding New Zealand's European beginnings, though linked to those of Australia, were a very different matter. No military-minded plan of punishment lay behind the first moves in the direction of these islands. During the mid-1790s, ships from the international sealing and whaling fleets began to work the seas near little-known New Zealand and Australia. Their crews' shore calls for fresh water, food, rest and repairs set up an occasional link between the two lands. Small groups of Maori sometimes sailed with the whalers or naval ships to visit Sydney. In this way Samuel Marsden came to meet and befriend several Maori of chiefly rank, and was impressed by their character and intelligence.

Marsden's interest in missionary activities was roused by the chance retreat to Sydney in 1798 of members of a mission to Tahiti, undertaken two years earlier. His contacts with Maori led him to see them as "a noble and intelligent race and prepared to receive the blessings of civilization and the knowledge of the Christian religion". He regarded them as more promising subjects for conversion than the "degraded" aborigines of New South Wales, more readily at hand.[3]

In 1808, during a three-year furlough visit to England, Marsden launched his bid for a New Zealand mission and obtained the Church Missionary Society's sanction to undertake it. With these beginnings, European intervention in New Zealand was about to commence.

Marsden was back in Sydney by 1810 with his first two artisan missionaries, one of whom, William Hall from Carlisle, would play an early role as a carpenter in our story of the New Zealand house. But the start was delayed nearly five years in recoil from the massacre of the *Boyd's* crew: the "noble savage" ideal had been shaken by the reality of fearsome cannibals.

Late in 1814 the mission at last set out for the Bay of Islands, secure enough in the support of some friendly Maori chiefs. They began to build at Rangihoua — the first settlement of European-style houses in New Zealand.[4]

Marsden's view of the missionary's role was a practical one. He believed the natives would more readily be persuaded to a Christian life after tasting the benefits of civilisation. The missionaries were to be artisans with constructive skills which they could teach the natives for their own industry; and those skills would also support the mission establishments in their virtual isolation.[5]

The mission succeeded in introducing Maori to crop production (wheat in particular), to iron tools (axes and hoes), and to literacy and other benefits of education. It also persuaded them to reduce significantly their cannibalistic activities. But during 15 years of evangelical effort, the natives remained steadfastly heathen. They had, however, become

A whare typifying Maori forms and construction with saplings and raupo reeds, as adopted by many Europeans for their first dwellings. (Drawing by L.A. de Sainson, 1827.) Low entries and sunken floors conserved warmth.

useful carpenters, brick makers and so forth. "It is by these people we get our work done," said Richard Davis, farming instructor.

In 1830 Marsden wrote of native carpenters at Paihia: "some of them can work very well as carpenters and will soon be able to build for themselves". By the mid-1830s the tide of conversion also turned. With the growing dependence of Maori on Europeans, their literacy and training in useful skills were seen to be creating a society of godly workmen.[6]

The mission houses

THE principal shaper of our first wooden houses on the Rangihoua mission hillside in 1815, and a key missionary in the spreading of the gospel and carpentry among the Maori, was the testy William Hall, carpenter and boat builder. The houses — simple thatched huts of saplings and bundled reeds — adapted Maori practices until sawpits were established later. By 1820 Hall, after five years at the mission, had been joined by three other carpenters whom Marsden had engaged in Sydney — three more Williams: Puckey (a Cornishman), Fairburn and Bean.

With the founding of missions at Kerikeri in 1819 and at Paihia in 1823, some of the first patterns for the New Zealand house in the next two decades were established. Of the houses built at Kerikeri and Paihia the only survivor is the substantial abode built for the Reverend John Butler in 1821–1822 — later occupied by James Kemp, blacksmith member of the initial band of artisan missionaries of 1814. However, plentiful drawings from the times give surprisingly accurate records of other houses in the early settlements. Together, these houses speak with some clarity and grace and with an assurance little expected when one considers that everything was wrought by hand tools in conditions akin to those of a desert island.

Their style has a stamp similar to that already seen in the New South Wales colony — and their common source is found in England's Georgian vernacular of the late 18th century.

Sydney preferred building in traditional brickwork, largely avoiding use of the difficult local hardwoods except for roof framing, shingles and farm buildings distant from kilns. But northern New Zealand was endowed with plentiful timber of the finest quality, readily worked. Our first carpenters therefore applied what little they knew of all-wooden construction, acquired in small part in Sydney but chiefly adapted from such familiarity as they had with certain English rural practices.

This starting point for New Zealand's wooden houses deserves a long look, bearing in mind what it presaged for the future. The shared origin of Sydney's and New Zealand's early wooden house style can be seen by a comparison of two characteristic early houses: Samuel Marsden's farm cottage at Parramatta outside Sydney, and the Butler–Kemp house at Kerikeri in the Bay of Islands. Both show a strong Georgian flavour and are clearly of the same family style. The elements of both designs are practically identical. At the back of Marsden's Parramatta house there was (eventually) a full outshoot under a "catslide" roof slope, while Butler's Kerikeri house ended up with a veranda around three sides and with lean-to additions at the back.

Given Marsden's connection with both houses it is tempting to see his hand in their design style. Yet, although acutely observant of people and occurrences, he seems to have been singularly blind to the appearance of buildings. Nowhere in his voluble journals does he comment on the style of any mission building. Indeed, he made the house a central issue in his acrimonious falling-out with the "vexatious" servant of the mission in 1823, scolding the Reverend Butler that this "very large and

10. *Kemp House, Kerikeri, Bay of Islands, 1821. Reverend John Butler's mission house is New Zealand's oldest surviving building. Blunt forms and small openings in the Georgian vernacular manner are similar in style to Marsden's cottage in Sydney (below). End verandas were added after 1840: all have since been rebuilt.*

10

11. *Kemp House, 1821. Butler's front door in "six panelled work. . . with a circular fanlight and pilasters" that irked William Hall. Beaded-edge weatherboards add to the worldly air of elegance.*

11   unnecessary building had been put up for him". No pride of design parentage there![7]

In fact the design of the house probably owes most to John Butler himself. Its form and general dimensions – even its rounded fanlight over the door – are close to those irritably described as "Butler's wishes" by William Hall (by now Superintendent of Public Works) in a letter written at the end of 1820. Butler had lived in Paddington, London, where he was accountant to a carrying firm until he became a missionary at age 37. He could have been as well informed about Georgian cottage styles in the villages and counties close to London, and as able to sketch them, as any expatriate carpenter.[8]

12   At the third mission, established at Paihia in 1823 by ex-Navy officer turned missionary of true calibre, Henry Williams, permanent houses were not begun until 1830. Two of them, shown in a drawing made by Richard Taylor in 1839, were of quite contrasting types: one in the old English tradition plus a colonial veranda, and the other a newer form derived from "colonial experience" worldwide. The Williams' parsonage, seen from in

12. *In* The Parsonage House, *Paihia, Bay of Islands, Reverend R. Taylor records two mission houses built c 1830. The distinctive roof shapes and screened verandas of both these important colonial house types recall sources in other cultures.*

front, has a blend of English rural forms in the current Georgian manner (a squatting, hip-roofed rectangle, with catslide outshoots at each end in the southeast-counties way) combined with a light, latticed veranda along the front, of Regency–Asian origins. The other house is directly "colonial" in all its forms; a square block whose pyramidal, tent-like roof sweeps out at a lesser slope over a deep, fully lattice-screened veranda on all four sides. It echoes antecedents somewhere else, in buildings for hot climates from India to the Caribbean and even Louisiana (see Chapter 5).[9]

At Waimate North, founded inland in 1831 as the fourth mission and a training station for Maori farmers, one house survives from three of matching design. Its layout and forms are similar to those of the Butler–Kemp house at Kerikeri but are lowered to one and a half storeys instead of two, with dormers in the hipped roof replacing windows in the upper walls. The Waimate house's proportions are thus quite different, lending the air of an Indian Service bungalow. In fact, though, its elements closely resemble those of the Paihia parsonage, on a larger scale.

The group of houses at Waimate was evidently planned by George Clarke, missionary blacksmith since 1824 turned carpenter (following his father's trade in Norfolk). They were largely constructed by mission-trained Maori carpenters. Charles Darwin in 1835 wrote approvingly of "the thoroughly English appearance of three well-designed respectable houses surrounded by gardens". Indeed today the stylish niceties of the Waimate and Kemp mission houses can be read as an aspiration to the life of gentry — above the "station" of humble missionaries, and incongruous in their remote island context. British airs and graces?[10]

Missionary carpenters and other settlers

THE English carpenters attached to the Church Missionary Society's settlements from 1815 on thus established New Zealand's early "main-

13. *Mission house, Waimate North, 1831. An expansive and handsome house, like the home of a country squire. Its forms contain elements from the mission houses at Kerikeri and Paihia, in a consistently developing style.*

13

11

stream" practices in wooden construction. The framing of their buildings followed medieval methods which had prevailed for centuries across the forested lands of England, France and Germany. They usually framed up walls with 3 in. (75 mm) thick studs spaced up to 3 ft. (900 mm) apart between heavy square main or corner posts. Studs were connected to levelled plates by laborious mortice-and-tenon joints worked in the solid, to minimise the use of nails: those that were used were expensive, being handmade by blacksmiths. A generation would pass before four-by-two timber framing, joined only by cheap, machine-cut nails, would be invented in the United States, eventually to be adopted universally.

Roof framing was often rudimentary, using halved or adzed saplings strutted up from walls. Trussed spans were uncommon in house roofs. Wall frames were generally lined with boarding, externally and internally. External planking was pit-sawn, a full inch (25 mm) in thickness to span adequately between studs, and usually lapped horizontally as weatherboards. Roofs were sometimes planked similarly; more commonly they were covered with split shingles (initially of ironbark imported from Sydney) fixed on close battening. Internally, walls, floors and ceilings (if any) were boarded, with edges butted or tongued together. In some cases traditional lath and plaster was used for interior linings, as in the Paihia mission houses.

From the mid-1820s, however, the mission carpenters were not alone in raising European-style buildings in subtropical Northland. A number of independent settlers gradually set up small communities around the Bay of Islands, where the white population by 1830 reached about 100, of whom at least half were the missionary families. "Europeans" —

14. *Mair homestead, Wahapu, Bay of Islands, 1830s. Behind its enclosing fence, the strong image of a distinctive early house type stands beautifully related to the crowning profile of the hill. Detail of a painting by J. Williams, c 1845.*

including Americans — were increasingly active in commercial whaling and trading operations, centred on the notorious Kororareka but also elsewhere.

Typical of these independent communities was the establishment of Gilbert Mair Snr, a ship's carpenter from near Aberdeen, Scotland, who came to New Zealand in 1824, worked briefly at Paihia for the CMS, then set up in business at Wahapu as a trader and ship repairer. Within a few years the shore was backed by a range of wooden buildings, with orderly and substantial workshops built by a Sydney carpenter. Mair erected his house on the hillside above, a truncated pyramidal roof over a single-storey core, rising from an embracing veranda on all sides — a constant early type. The first exports of kauri gum to the United States were made by trader Mair in about 1838 (followed by James Busby), establishing a long-lasting trade and an early social connection with America. **14**

Another independent was James Clendon, resident since 1832 in his trading post at Okiato. Hailing originally from Kent, he had made trading visits as a British shipowner and master to Hokianga from 1828. He also had connections with Yankee whaling ships about this time — which will bring us back to him later, at Kororareka.[11]

Although Marsden ruled the missions of the CMS by remote control — in seven visits from Sydney over 23 years, he spent in total about two years in New Zealand — his presence hovers like a vengeful angel over the whole precolonial period. In 1831, it was he who recommended to Governor Darling that a British Resident be stationed in New Zealand to bring some legal authority into the depraved conditions at the Bay of Islands — conditions caused by the growth of international shipping and exploitation of Maori by Europeans. Subsequently, in 1832, James Busby was appointed in a limited attempt to introduce some control.

Of particular interest is the house that accompanied Busby from Sydney, the modest Georgian bungalow which he built at Waitangi in 1833. Most familiar of all our precolonial houses, the so-called Treaty House stands today as a much-extended and restored building of higher finish than the initial Residency. Its taller, more formal stance than that of the homespun mission houses, and the elegance of its proportions, attest to the sophisticated hand of Busby's leading Sydney architect, John Verge, at work in the formal style current for official buildings. But the French doors and veranda equally indicate its lineage in the "colonial experi- **15**

15. *Busby Residency (architect: J. Verge), Waitangi, Bay of Islands, 1833. The prominent front block contains the original two large rooms flanking a lobby, with a shallow but dignified veranda, much as it began.*

ence" then running as a thread through the Georgian–Regency style in England.

The dignified grace of this New Zealand icon, though, conceals its niggardly beginnings. Busby's authority was given minimal support. The governor had Verge's plan reduced, and supplied the house as a precut frame with fittings and most other materials. Poor, dutiful Busby had to pay the cost of freight to New Zealand as well as his own passage — *and for land on which to build!*[12]

Kororareka

BUSBY'S well-bred house would hardly set the norm for the common man's house. But across the bay the nascent boom town of Kororareka was rapidly acquiring an assemblage of house types closer to that image.

Kororareka (the present-day Russell) was important as New Zealand's first trading port and first European "town" from the early 1830s — a frontier settlement where many nationalities mixed, without established law or government. Through the 1830s, "the decade of a thousand ships", the population grew in response to the increasing patronage of whaling vessels, calling for shore rest, fresh water, female recreation, pork and repairs. Kororareka was notorious worldwide for its mix of grog shops, brothels, deserters, runaway convicts, raiding Maori and general debauchery — a cutthroat, lawless hellhole. But there were also ship chandlers, traders' agents, hoteliers, merchants' stores, restaurants, even a French bishop's headquarters and a "respectable" part of town.

British, French and American whaling fleets had been working the South Pacific since the early 1800s, attracted by the twice-yearly migration of whales past New Zealand. They sought whale oil for lamps and as a lubricant for the early machines of the industrial revolution. By the late 1830s, United States whalers, based at Nantucket or New Bedford on the American East Coast, made up the majority of visiting ships. Their crews no doubt contributed their share to the general mayhem which made Kororareka famous.

This major American presence in the Bay of Islands led to the appointment in 1839 of James Clendon, resident at Okiato, as New Zealand's first United States consul, primed by his earlier dealings with Yankee captains. Clendon looked after the interests of American residents

16. *Kororareka, Bay of Islands, 1844. Edward Ashworth, architect–artist, drew this tiny panorama across the foot of his sketchbook pages: a meticulous depiction of many of our earliest building types (actual size).*

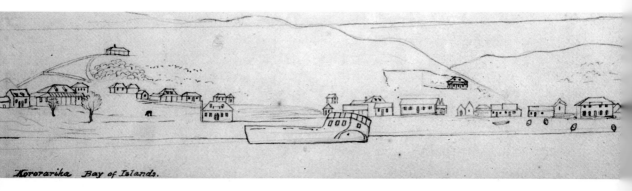

Kororareka. Bay of Islands.

and represented US law among the American sailors until mid-1841. Clearly, the American connection with New Zealand began early.

In the 1830s French interest was also marked, just when British whalers' activity was in the minority. French whalers, merchants and traders, setting up in Kororareka prior to Bishop Pompallier's mission, gave further colour to the international melange. It is evident that the many-nationed whalers' presence in "the Bay" created most of the pressures that led to the annexation of New Zealand as a British colony in 1840.[13]

Equally multicultural was the polyglot range of house types and shapes lining the shore in New Zealand's first European town. In contrast to the orderly mission houses and traders' settlements, this "town" was a disjointed array strung in loose clusters along the beach. But here were the first intimations of many strands of overseas influence in our early house forms. Very little remains today: the whaling activity declined, and Hone Heke and his men sacked and razed the wooden town in 1845, sparing only mission buildings and churches.

One day in the previous year, fortunately for us, artist Edward **16** Ashworth sat on a ship moored off shore and sketched a panorama of the bay's sweep, leaving us a catalogue of house and building types. His accurate architect's eye ranged past folk-style cottages, taverns and lodgings, two of the more substantial hotels, two churches, stores, houses of ill repute, a mini Waimate house in a hillside garden, round to the French mission with its dominant, flared printery roof.

Among the builders of this settlement were a few Scottish artisans, some of whom had settled as early as 1826, some carpenters and sawyers over from Sydney, and mission-trained Maori carpenters whose productive work was by now widely employed on settlers' houses as well as on their own native buildings. Folk-type houses with their economical geometry are here joined by more informed adaptations of houses known to suit hot climates. Seafarers' knowledge, gathered from ports of call around the world, was added to the pool of the tradesman's traditional lore.

The contribution made to our early house types by seafarers' knowledge, gleaned from foreign parts, was without doubt significant. In the 1830s, local builders were outnumbered a hundredfold by carpenters on visiting ships. The "thousand ships" (all wooden) each had at least one carpenter on board. Many stayed for lengthy periods ashore; some settled after deserting from the long voyages of two to four years' duration.

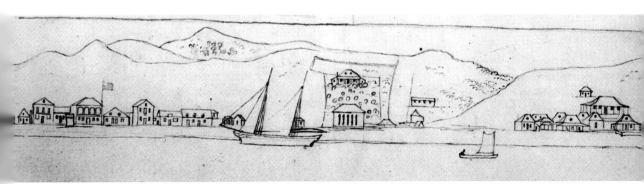

Portsmouth, Jamaica, Calcutta, St Domingue, Nantucket, New Orleans — all were within the experience of early 19th-century seagoers. The diversity of building types along Kororareka's shore reflected the range of experience in the carpenters' interpretations of house forms from other climatic zones and countries, with lasting effect on the shapes of our indigenous houses.

In Ashworth's drawing of Kororareka, and in other topographical depictions from the same time (including C. Pharazyn's painting of 1843), a number of distinct early house types can be identified:

1. Scattered cottages have the fully hipped, low roof recognisable as the typical English Georgian rural form, prevalent in the southeast counties and seen in the New South Wales colony.

2. Back on the hillside are houses of Georgian colonial type, familiar from the missions, with a front veranda and dormers in the roof, and with hints of the Indian Service bungalow.

3. At the far southern end (to the right in Ashworth's drawing) is a cluster of about eight houses in a French colonial manner — not only the Pompallier printery of 1842 but also an earlier group, built by local speculator Ben Turner in 1838. They have higher-pitched hipped roofs than the Georgians, and some splay out over verandas on three sides, with small dormers high up in the roof. Here are distinct echoes of West Indies plantation houses, of St Domingue and New Orleans.

4. To the left of the schooner are the closed forms of traditional gable-ended, joint-row cottages (built by the Scotsmen, perhaps), with dormers straight above the wall face in the usual British way.

5. A two-storeyed building further left, possibly a major hotel, has an impressive colonnaded gallery under its hipped roof, strongly reminiscent of Jamaica's shaded galleries on street fronts of the 1800s. Adding a piquant reminder of the international flavour of the time is the flag flying from the building's mast — the Stars and Stripes of the United States consul.

In C. Pharazyn's watercolour sketch are several houses with the slanting side profile of New England's "salt-box" houses — influence, perhaps, of the Nantucket-based whalers. The roof of the high, gable-ended front block carries down over a rear "skilling" or full-width lean-to, resembling an old-fashioned salt container.

At this early time, then, our first town brought together types of houses from a much wider orbit than Old England alone. Models came also from the modern colonial world, houses better suited to life in a sultry climate, and shaped by the easy use of fine timber such as was no longer plentiful "at home".

In 1840, when Captain Hobson established British sovereignty over

New Zealand at Waitangi, he purchased Clendon's house at Okiato as the first seat of government. But within a year he moved the capital of the new colony to Auckland, and shipped 32 tradesmen down from the Bay of Islands as a building team (the "mechanics" who are remembered in the name given to the bay where they were lodged).

These carpenters, smiths and bricklayers brought with them from Kororareka their experiences of the international origins of New Zealand's first common houses, and made of them a basis for their building activities in the fledgling Auckland.

Edward Ashworth, again, in a drawing made in the town in 1843, shows that the houses they built were not simply like those they had known "at home" in Britain. These, with their encircling verandas and French windows, speak of much hotter climes. And even at this early date, they bear the unmistakable stamp of what was to become one of our commonest Victorian houses, about to be repeated by the thousand.

17. *Commercial Bay, Auckland, 1843: an ink-and-wash drawing by Edward Ashworth which indicates the early presence in towns of the familiar four-square, peak-roofed and fully verandaed Victorian cottage.*

17

Chapter 3

British Sources

A wooden heritage

NEW Zealand has always been a land of wooden houses. Its nearest neighbour Australia, on the other hand, has built its houses predominantly in brick. New Zealand is comparable only with North America and Scandinavia as a modern-age timber-rich land populated by wooden-house dwellers.

This description certainly does not match the typical image of Britain. Yet the first European-type houses built by British settlers in New Zealand were wooden framed and weatherboarded. Our purpose here is to locate the source of this initial practice and to unravel some of the influences bearing upon it.

Despite indications to the contrary, Britain does have a tradition of timber-framed and weatherboarded rural buildings other than houses. In the southeast counties of England, great country barns and water mills — even windmills and the occasional church tower — were for centuries built in heart of oak in a strongly functional tradition of wooden construction. "Heart of oak" is a reminder of the timber-related crafts of shipbuilding; and in the new industrial buildings of the late 1700s, both nautical and rural skills were combined in bold wooden constructions for textile mills, dockyard sheds, factories and small warehouses.

"The anonymous idiom of the shipwright," wrote J.M. Richards in 1957, "introduced into this architecture that combination of toughness, neatness and economy of conception encountered in everything connected with the sea." Akin to the lapped boards of clinker-built boats, the simplest form of weatherboarding, generally painted white, was widely used on the walls of these industrial buildings.[1]

As for England's wooden houses, we do know them, of course, from

18

18. *A water-mill granary, Bocking, Essex, 18th century. The functional vernacular of rural buildings is evident in the clean geometry, versatile construction, freely placed openings and white weatherboarding.*

medieval times as the heavy, half-timbered Tudor structures panelled with brick or plaster infilling. But weatherboarded houses are a different matter: they play only a minor part in the story and are generally regarded as an oddity. In his book *The English House* (1959), Robert Furneaux Jordan describes a centuries-old timber-framed cottage in Kent as "a curious survival of an economical form of structure . . . covered with weatherboarding on the ground floor and hung with tiles on the upper floor. Nevertheless it is sound and weatherproof . . . " Alec Clifton-Taylor, writing on building materials in *The Buildings of England: Surrey* (1962), finds it "amusing . . . that weatherboarded cottages still survive in a number of places that have now become urban or suburban". Others see weatherboarding as "temporary", "suitable only for farm buildings and minor cottages", or even "uncouth", sharing a stigma much like that of using "industrial" corrugated iron on domestic walls.

Nevertheless, from around the 1760s in the southeastern counties near London and into Essex, weatherboarding was used locally on houses, both

Pl. 6

19

19. *Rolvenden, Kent, 18th century. A row of half-timber-framed cottages, protected from the elements by a later surfacing of brick and weatherboarding.*

Pl. 7

as weatherproofing over old and leaky half-timbered walls from the past and as a covering for new houses. The practice was centred on Kent and Sussex with their age-old timber traditions. This district of the Weald, once densely forested, had supplied oak for the British Navy in Elizabethan times; and the coastal perimeter from Portsmouth around to the Thames estuary had for centuries been steeped in seafaring ways and customs. It was a region stimulated by the presence of great naval shipbuilding yards with their wood-based prowess, coloured by the daring of smugglers, and busy nurturing carpenters who were as much at home at sea as on land. Perhaps it was with these factors in mind that Batsford and Fry, referring in *The English Cottage* (1938) to the use of weatherboarding on cottage walls, wrote "there seems some curious connection between this practice and coastal districts".[2]

That it was not a widespread English practice is evident from the lack of attention given to the topic in books on traditional building methods. In *Old English Country Cottages*, a study of some 170 pages edited by Charles Holme for *The Studio* in 1906, no more than ten lines deal with weatherboarded cottages — even within the chapter on Kent, Surrey and Sussex, where the method was quite common.

The southeast counties are distinguished for the blending, during the late 1700s, of their traditional forms of rural houses with the fashionable Georgian style, then in vogue all over England. The style sought a unity of design through formal symmetry and regular repetition of windows in plain walls, usually of brick or stone. But the introduction, in these southeastern counties, of walls in white-painted weatherboarding gave the style

Pl. 1 *(above) Residential street in Bournville, Birmingham. Post-Victorian middle-class uniformity in brick: constraints on one's individual space are imposed and accepted. Urban indoor living, the two-dimensional facades preserving a private world within.*

Pl. 2 *(right) Residential street in Lagos de Moreno, Mexico. The faceless wall of introvert privacy. This ancient form of enclosed courtyard house occurs everywhere in the Arab and Spanish worlds. In contrast is the extrovert life in the street.*

Pl. 3 *(left) Hill suburb in Ngaio, Wellington. Individual liberty in one's own space is found and accepted. Pursuit of the outdoor life, close to the land and nature.*

Pl. 4 *(bottom left) Hill suburb at Silver Lake, Los Angeles. Individual liberty in one's own space is claimed and asserted. Pursuit of the outdoor life, aware of the land and nature.*

Pl. 5 *(right) Cliff village, Mesa Verde, Colorado. Homes of Anasazi Indians, built beneath a rock shelf, c 1250. As formerly in ancient Jericho, rectangular order prevailed here; but circular forms endured in* kivas *for cult ceremonies.*

Pl. 6 *(right) Half-timber living quarters built onto Stokesay Castle, Shropshire, c 1280, provided privacy for the lord's family away from the public Great Hall. Beautiful in form and proportion, they achieved a modern domestic quality in one brilliant step. Present windows are 17th century.*

Pl. 7 *(left) English yeoman's house, Northiam, East Sussex. A latter-18th-century weatherboarded version of a timber-framed type common in the 17th century, with end lean-to added. It probably always had casement windows.*

Pl. 8 *(below) Farmhouse, Iden, near Rye, East Sussex, early 18th century, rebuilt late 18th century. Exemplifying the assurance of the Georgian vernacular style, this broad-windowed brick and half-timber-framed house near Kent is tile-hung on its upper walls.*

20. *Osborne House, High Street, Bexhill, East Sussex. Late 18th-century Georgian formality lives happily with rural roof forms, as does local clapboarding with white stucco, lined out as stonework.*

a distinctive twist. Its quality was appreciated by Olive Cook in her *English House Through Seven Centuries*: "There is no more delightful version of the Georgian style than the wood-framed, clapboarded houses of southeastern England, particularly of Kent where . . . trim, symmetrical structures front the high streets with a distinctly nautical air." And of weatherboarding she wrote further: "the emphatically horizontal aspect it imparts to a facade was peculiarly suited to the Georgian and Regency house". By the early 1800s, this individual version of the smaller Georgian house had become locally the "in" thing — at the very time of the founding of Australia and New Zealand.

20

In his great standard work *The History of the English House*, Nathaniel Lloyd wrote in 1931: "So popular did wall tiling and weatherboarding become that for small houses and cottages they may be said to have been

21. *Northiam, East Sussex. This farm group has the ingenuous charm of the Wealden weatherboarded vernacular. Roof forms and wall patterns are handled with casual ease.*

the predominant building materials of the period between 1750 and 1850 in the eastern and southern counties." Of weatherboarding specifically, Batsford and Fry in 1938 noted its prevalence was most marked "in the sandy Weald extending from Tunbridge Wells to Rye", a distance of a mere 30 miles (50 km). Indeed, to this day within a band a dozen miles wide, straddling the border shared by East Sussex and Kent, lie a score or so villages with many charming white weatherboarded houses sheltering **21** under trim roofs of red burnt clay tiles, seemingly unchanged after two centuries. To New Zealand eyes they look pleasantly familiar.

Batsford and Fry identified one other English locality where weatherboarding was frequently found on cottages. This lay in southern Essex — that part of East Anglia directly across the Thames estuary from Kent. Georgian simplicity governed as in Kent, but Essex favoured end walls with gables rather more than a hipped roof.[3]

Taking the southeast as a whole, it is evident that the region's house style — in its unselfconscious approach, vocabulary of design forms, and details of wooden construction — shows a marked similarity to early pioneering houses in New Zealand. It may seem presumptuous to indicate Sussex and Kent in particular as the main source of forms and style adopted in New Zealand's first generation of common houses, yet the evidence points firmly in that direction.

Early patterns for New Zealand

THE first style introduced by our British forebears, in both Australia and New Zealand around the 1800s, is typified by two of the earlier houses: **9** the Reverend Samuel Marsden's government-built cottage near Sydney **10** and the mission-built Kemp House for the Reverend John Butler in the Bay of Islands. Their parental character is classic in spirit, in the Georgian vernacular manner, and weatherboarded. Both houses are calm in proportions, symmetrical, and have straight eaves lines under a simple hipped roof. Windows, regularly spaced, are either double-hung sashes of Georgian style or the earlier casement type.

22. *Guestling, near Hastings, East Sussex. Paired cottages with hipped roofs and full rear extensions, weatherboarded all over, which combine the same elements as the basic colonial Marsden and Kemp houses.*

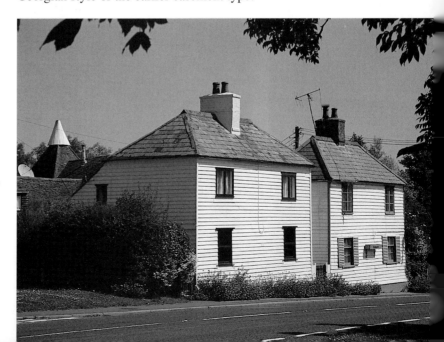

This simple catalogue is repeated in many early New Zealand houses. It matches the common style of Georgian rural houses in the districts where Sussex and Kent meet — those houses which were enjoying a fashionable popularity locally at the time.

    22

In the rest of Britain during the same period, houses and cottages were built in many materials other than wood. There were marked traditional differences to be seen between groups of counties, due to their own history, their forests and geology. In most counties, medieval half-timber construction had gone out of favour by the early 1700s, partly through exhaustion of the oak forests, but also in being outmoded by the superior comfort of the new houses in brick and stone. In East Anglia, Sussex and Kent, however, the tradition of construction in wood continued to dominate the common man's house. Increasingly, for economic reasons, softwoods were imported from the Baltic and America, and were used for framing in smaller sizes than before and for weatherboarding, in a local revival of an old practice. Alec Clifton Taylor, in writing of the building materials of Kent, noted that "Weatherboarding occurs more often in the Weald of Kent than perhaps anywhere else in the country."

The bold all-hipped roofs of Kent were a further characteristic of these parts, rare elsewhere on cottages. (Even dormer windows had their own miniature hipped roofs, a practice native to this region.) The normal roof type in English cottage history has been the gabled form, the hipped roof being a late introduction. G.L. Morris, in *Old English Country Cottages*, writes: "With the exception of the county of Kent, the gable predominates everywhere . . . the wholly-hipped roof being rare in comparison with the other form." Batsford and Fry also refer to "the hips of the South East".[4]

The hipped roof was one of the principal components of the national Georgian style in the "polite" great houses — with grand precedents in Wren's Renaissance architecture. But it happened to be also the traditional Kentish roof form for centuries. As a result, Kentish practices lent themselves to a felicitous merging of the rustic and the sophisticated, well developed by provincial builders in their more modest houses for local pastors, farmers and county squires.

    8

    Pl. 8

This rural Kentish version of the Georgian style clearly provided one of the main streams from which early New Zealand basic houses were derived, including most of the mission houses. The type relates directly to

    23

23. *Northiam, East Sussex. A more sophisticated Georgian wooden house of simple cubic form, with rear extension. The bay window is a Victorian addition.*

24. *Bell House, Howick, Auckland, 1852, home of Captain M. Smith. British army officers were sometimes provided with orderly, well-proportioned houses, free from affectation and serving as sensible models for others.*

24

the folk-form rectangular hut or cabin, with a central door between a pair of windows. This simple hip-roofed, weatherboarded, symmetrical wooden house, usually shingle roofed with almost no eaves and often bare walled without verandas, became the common man's home in our early settlements. The form persisted everywhere as the core of later developments and variants for decades. Yet English precedent for its dual distinguishing features of weatherboarded walls and all-hipped roof are found in combination only in the southeast counties, especially in Kent and East Sussex.

In this simple and currently popular style our British settlers, missionaries and immigrants had available a ready-made answer for their new houses in timber-rich New Zealand. These first New Zealand wooden houses have an appealing quality of domesticity, offering a pleasant image of a relaxing home. Readily followed and not too demanding of craftsmanship, this "Kentish-style" house would have been familiar to most in the south of England a century and a half ago, including naval and other seafarers — and to their ships' carpenters.

The fact that Kent was a major source of the New Zealand Company's settlers for its first towns of Wellington and Nelson in the 1840s may simply have strengthened this adherence.

Chapter 4

Clapboards, Old Saws and Know-how

The weatherboard family tree

A characterful hallmark of the colonial New Zealand house must surely be its weatherboards, long taken for granted without a thought for the origins of their use.

Horizontal lapped boarding is known to have been used in England for weather protection on walls well before 1540, when the word *whetherborde* is first recorded. Before the early 1700s, however, use of weatherboards had not developed beyond minor applications to the sides of farm buildings, the occasional church tower, pockets of Pepysian London before the Fire, and a few cottage gables in the southeast.

The family from which our ordinary tilt-lapped weatherboards are descended has many branches. One of the more significant lines of development, from a New Zealand viewpoint, stems from the founding of the American colonies in the 17th century.

When the first settlers landed in 1607 at the site of England's earliest colony, Virginia, on America's Atlantic coast, they found great forests of hardwood oaks resembling the oaks of England. Indeed, one of the prospects intended for the new colony was to supply timber to England, where oak forests and other hardwoods had been seriously depleted in the building of the Royal Navy of Henry VIII and Elizabeth I, as well as by profligate use of massive timbers in houses and other buildings. (In the event, it was the tobacco weed that made the new colonists' fortunes.)

In Virginia, and later in New England, the colonists built as their fathers had — in the medieval tradition of half-timber construction.

Pl. 6

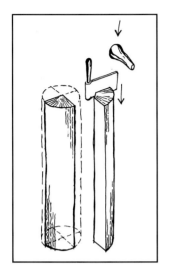

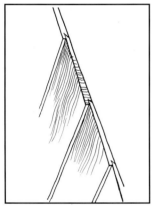

The frameless pitsaw had a broad, long blade thrust vertically by two sawyers, one of them called the pitman, the other the top-notcher (from the notches he cut to mark the cutting lines).

Heavy timber frames of posts and beams were locked together by pegged tenon joints. Smaller uprights, between the main posts, supported infilling panels of soft brickwork or of clay-mud on woven twigs in the wall spaces. But it was soon evident that this north European walling system could not stand up to the severity of America's Atlantic-side climate. The extremes of heat, cold and gale-driven rain, which made English conditions seem mild by comparison, sought out every gap between cracked panels and shrinking woodwork. Drastic measures were needed to overcome the leakages; and the colonists, poorly equipped with tools and skills, turned their attention to available natural resources.[1]

They found no lime for plaster coating of the walls, as was done in England for protection. Even if they knew of the occasional use of weatherboarding in parts of England, their medieval framed pitsaws were inadequate for ripping hard oak into wide boards without excessive use of time and labour. However, they did know an age-old method by which thin staves of oak could be split off short lengths of log. The upended log was split along its radial lines by driving a wedge blade downwards, producing "feather edge" tapered boards up to 5 ft. long (1.5 m). Known as *clapboards* since about 1520, such staves had been used in Europe only internally for partitions, set up vertically with their edges interlocked. This resulted in a slightly saw-toothed profile on the boarded surface.

From this method, out of necessity, the American settlers invented a solution for the problem of their leaking walls by adapting these short clapboards to serve as a weatherproof cladding on their houses. They lapped and fixed them *horizontally*, as weatherboards, the simple overlaps producing a serrated profile like that of internal clapboarding. (And, commencing less than a year after the first landing, lightly laden ships returning to England carried cargoes of oak clapboards as ballast, both from Virginia and, after 1620, from New England.)[2]

Hardwoods were worked from early times in America, but further exploration soon opened up stands of softwoods such as white and yellow pine, cedar and poplar. Weatherboards of greater width and length could now be sawn readily from softwood logs and were universally adopted. Eventually, the term *clapboarding* was to come into general use right across America, applying equally to sawn horizontal exterior boarding of all kinds. The widespread use of wooden cladding on timber-framed buildings was the first significant adaptation of traditional English building methods to American conditions, as R. Brunskill pointed out in his *Illustrated Handbook of Vernacular Architecture* in 1971.[3]

By the mid-1600s, improved frameless pitsaws were being used. However, the English authorities soon set up many water-powered sawmills, often with two or three framed pitsaws joined as a gang saw, to increase production for export. With sawmills in full action from early in the 1630s, a range of excellent timbers was available to the colonists as well as to England for shipbuilding and house construction.

From that time forward in the American colonies, through the 1600s and early 1700s, our modern form of weatherboarding was being developed aided by the availability of durable softwoods and improved

saw utilisation. It was largely due to the absence in England of both of these factors that the use of weatherboarding there had been severely limited since its late medieval origins. Although sawmills were common in Europe there was none in England by 1660; but "hundreds" were in use in America. Social concerns about unemployment led to the removal of England's first water-driven mill during the 1660s, prevented another in 1700, and saw a mob of sawyers destroy one even in 1767.[4]

Between 1640 and 1700, the characteristic forms of the early American colonial wooden house were established. Forthright, even plain, one-and-a-half- and two-storeyed houses, more or less symmetrical with large, sharp-lined flush gables and small, grouped casements (or, later, the new sash windows), they were entirely clad in mill-sawn, unpainted, horizontally lapped weatherboards. Wooden houses quite outnumbered those built of brick; and in general, houses were larger-scaled than their English counterparts.

25

To the eyes of New Zealanders of the 1850s, the shapes and materials of these pre-1700 American houses would have looked familiar! A description of them by Talbot Hamlin, American historian, as having all the "charm of sincere effort, naive ignorance and unskilful execution" could have fitted many of the early New Zealand houses as well, no doubt.[5]

Of course, the concealed heavy-timber framework of the American houses and their strong gabled forms were English derived; but their fully boarded exteriors were of a character rarely seen in England. There, through the 1600s, weatherboarding of whole houses from new, as done in America, was not normal practice anywhere. In the absence of usable softwoods in Britain's forests, planks of any length had to be split laboriously out of hardwood balks by axe or wedge, then adzed. By about 1650 the frameless pitsaw had been developed; nevertheless, sawing oak logs of ironlike hardness remained unrelentingly onerous and costly. Use of weatherboards could probably be justified for higher parts of structures where a lightweight cladding was needed, as on church towers, occasional gables, and windmills; but costs would have been prohibitive for the family house. Weatherboards were not cheap.

Wider use of weatherboards in England would remain impracticable until well into the 1700s, when water-powered sawmills, already proven in America, were belatedly put to work (not without social resistance, as noted). By then, supplies of suitable pine, poplar or deal softwoods were being imported from the American colonies as well as from Scandinavia.

Fashionable weatherboards in England

THE colonists in Virginia and New England were not, as it happened, the only ones to have trouble with leaking traditional half-timbered walls. Similar problems were arising with England's valuable but ageing stock of half-timber-and-panel houses from previous centuries (see Chapter 3). Now, in the 1700s, their leaks and draughts were no longer acceptable alongside the levels of comfort reached by the newer brick houses of the rising merchant class. Nor were leaks their only drawback: their wooden bones, too, were looking outdated in the calm climate of the new early Georgian style.

In East Anglia and other parts of England many half-timbered houses had, during the previous century, been given a smooth coating of lime plaster across their whole wall surface as a protection against the elements, concealing their framework and thus blandly updating them as well. The southeastern counties, however, had always looked to the bountiful local wood for their building needs, and they found the remedy

19 for their leaking old houses in a revitalised adoption of weatherboarding.[6]

The introduction of sawmills and softwoods had gradually changed the availability of weatherboards from about the 1730s, and enabled England to expand the practice — perhaps, we may wonder, by following the American precedents? By midcentury the use of weatherboarding had

18 increased, at first on new farm structures, water mills and windmills around and to the southeast of London. Later, it came into favour as a protective cladding on the old-fashioned half-timbered houses themselves.

It is of considerable interest that the colonists of America who, a hundred years before, had revived and then developed weatherboarding as their universal practice, came predominantly from those same areas of East Anglia and the southeast counties; and it was in that part of England,

26. *Georgian house near Rolvenden, Kent, c 1780. A localised vogue for white, weatherboarded new houses arose in the southeast counties from about 1780 to the 1820s — coinciding with the founding of Australia and New Zealand.*

and only there, that a wide interest in using weatherboards was awakened around 1750. Indeed, in the last quarter of the century fully weatherboarded white-painted houses, new as well as resurfaced old, became a popular feature of those parts. But in America white-painted weatherboarded houses had been a major standardised type through the whole century, refined in the distinctive American Colonial style from about 1710.

26

27

Could it be that continued interchange between friends and family on both sides of the Atlantic, throughout the colonial period, had ensured knowledge in England of the Americans' house-building methods? Perhaps this contact fostered use of the American system of softwood weatherboarding and its details. American timber had by now been imported to England for well over 100 years: how could the know-how of its usage have been left behind?

These American colonials, moreover, had adapted the technique into presentable versions of Wren and early Georgian house tradition, translated from masonry to wood. Although little removed from an untutored vernacular idiom, their attractive houses were abreast of London in the use of double-hung sash windows and moulded doorways. Furthermore, their tidy design and crisp detailing showed that wooden houses were capable of "respectability". They had been developing the vocabulary of weatherboarding consistently for a century or more.

Weatherboarding dialects

THE detail language of a weatherboarding style shows itself at the interruptions to the walling and in the ways they are handled. These junctions, at corners and at door and window openings, differ widely among countries and cultures.

At first, in the American colonies from about 1630 to the century's end, the details at corners were both rudimentary and sturdy — as was the unpainted boarding itself. Wide, vertical cover boards were sometimes lapped both ways on top of the weatherboard ends; but more frequently

25

the weatherboards were butted into the edge of thicker corner boards in a near-flush finish. (The former method, relatively bulky, has been widely used on New Zealand homes for many years, but appears infrequently in England.) Since sawn weatherboards usually did not match in their widths, these corners allowed boards on adjoining walls to run "out of step". (Mitring of the boards at corners would have been rare.) At doors and casement windows, weatherboards were usually butted against the frame (or a small facing) with all the outer edges lying flush, and with no cover board over the junction.

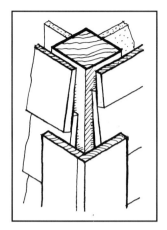

Cover boards.

From the 1700s, more refined solutions to these unavoidable details of wood construction were achieved independently in America, particularly at corners — ever-prominent to the eye.

First, in a refinement adopted in Virginia, the pair of near-flush corner boards was superseded by using only the wider of the pair, as a single, vertical corner stop about 3 by $1^1/_2$ in. (75 by 40 mm), set practically flush. The resulting character was unemphatic, trim and elegant. (The

28

same detail was used through New Zealand's first 50 years or so, a century later.)[7]

A second, more common, refinement was made at window openings, following adoption of the Georgian style of double-hung sashes. The faces of the weight boxes were neatly covered by the weatherboarding, which stopped against a small facing at the edge of the opening in the same way as at corner stops.

A third element of change, widely adopted from about 1720, introduced the painting of weatherboarding and sashes with white lead in oil, which scientists had found would give softwoods some weather protection (which oak and cedar had not required).

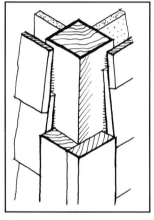

Near-flush corner boards.

All three of these refinements, present in Virginian houses of the early 1700s, later emerged in an expanded use of weatherboarding around Essex, Sussex and Kent a little before 1750, at first on rural buildings, and on houses somewhat later (see illustrations, Chapter 3).

From the New to the Old?

IN his *Early American Architecture*, in 1952, Hugh Morrison noted that contact between England and the American South had been close by way of the busy ships carrying tobacco direct to London: "Thus it was easy, in fashions, manners, and in architecture, to keep in close touch with the mother country." It doubtless worked as a two-way exchange of know-how, at least before the bid for independence of 1776.

Might the enterprising New World have thus given back to the Old World the archaic weatherboard in a modern guise? It seems that the down-to-earth builders of Kent and Sussex may indeed have taken a lead from

29

their American cousins. Certainly by the mid-1700s weatherboards had been adopted widely as never before, white-painted and with the identical trim detailing at corners and window edges that had been in use in America for decades. Comparative evidence is abundant in the houses themselves — even if English versions generally remained at a level of relative naivety and quaintness when compared with the sophisticated finish and orderliness of the common American houses.[8]

This possible chain of connection does not seem to have been widely noticed — perhaps because of the barriers of nationalist viewpoints. But it is a linkage of particular interest in New Zealand's story, as our adoption of Kentish-type weatherboarding would have introduced the earliest instance of American precedent, woven into our British inheritance as an indirect thread.

It appears likely that American advances in weatherboarding during their colonial period set a pattern on which southeastern England further developed its usages; and that from there, in New Zealand's earliest days, we adopted those practices — including all three distinctive features defined above. It might be recalled that weatherboarded houses had reached their popular vogue in Sussex and Kent between the 1780s and 1820s, at the same time that the antipodean colonies were taking shape.[9]

28. *Plain 3 by 2 in. (75 by 50 mm) corner stops were the normal corner finish for "tilt-lapped" weatherboards in New Zealand until c 1870, when flat, rusticated boarding prevailed with lapped cover boards instead.*

30

Beadings and dormers

ALONGSIDE the refinements already described as characteristic of early American wooden houses, three other items from Virginia are of particular interest to us. Basic to two of them is the use of a small, rounded edge-beading, usually ⅝ in. (16 mm) in diameter, formed by running a moulding plane along the corner of boards, frames and finishings. Its use was so general that Marcus Whiffen, in *The Eighteenth Century Houses*

29. *Quaker's Mill granary and house, Bexhill, East Sussex, 18th century. Early industrial relics (with additions), whose weatherboarding shares details with American practices.*

30. *Water of Leith mill and brewery, Dunedin, 1865 and 1861 (right). Orderly and well-proportioned forms in the industrial wooden vernacular,* **27** *learnt from the south and east of England. The same trimness of detail appears on early houses.*

of Williamsburg, called it "the hallmark of colonial work in Virginia". Two exterior applications of this beading are of note: first, as a beaded lip run on the bottom edge of each weatherboard, making a doubled shadow line; and second, as a beaded corner run up the edge of vertical corner stops. The third item concerns the practice of fixing weatherboarding *diagonally* on the side walls of dormers, at the same slope as the roof — a method apparently peculiar to the American South for standard dormer windows from about 1700.

Now beadings themselves were no invention: they were ages old on panelling, frames and other interior joinery work in England. This use in Virginia, though, was as a universal exterior refinement, on boarded houses. Again, I have found no indication of a similar practice of fixing boarding diagonally on dormer cheeks in England.

It comes as a surprise, then, to encounter all three of these particular details, reproduced as at Williamsburg, among several of New Zealand's oldest houses dating from mission and earliest colonial days in the north, when such sophistication would be least expected. Beaded weatherboards **10** enhance the walls of the Kemp house at Kerikeri (1821), Busby's 1833 **31, 32** residence and its wings (1842) at Waitangi, and the mission house at Waimate North (1831), while bead-edged corner stops were used on **32** many corners of all three. (Three-quarter-round staff beads or quarter- **31** round inset stops — of dubious weatherproofness — were used at others.)

From the same period, weatherboards fixed diagonally appear on dor- **33** mer cheeks of some mission houses, as at Mangungu (1839 — or 1855, when rebuilt at Onehunga) and The Elms in Tauranga (1846), as well as **46** at Scoria House (St Keven's) in Auckland (1847). At Kororareka (now Russell) they are on the dormers of James Clendon's "Bungalow" of the 1850s, and were recently, for a time, on the Pompallier printery nearby — suggesting a local idiom of some standing. Other examples are known further south, from the 1850s in Dunedin's main street, in 1870s Wellington and in Akaroa.

Marcus Whiffen (from England) saw those American colonial dormers to be a "prime example of a feature that acquired distinctively Virginia forms". He observed that "Virginia dormers had noticeably taller proportions than their counterparts in England" and that certain characteristics "isolated them as a singular class"; namely, their diagonally boarded cheeks and their peaked roofs of similar slope to the main roof. Surprisingly, New Zealand examples are virtually the same as those of early Williamsburg in their tall proportions, gabled roof peak and sloping boarded cheeks. Even double-hung Georgian sashes in the dormers are directly comparable, in being scaled down to about three-quarters of the window size on the main floor.[10][11]

In the Bay of Islands during the 1830s, United States ships and crews outnumbered those of any other nation. Who knows what American eastern seaboard ideas were transmitted to our building traditions by their ship's carpenters during their off-season months on shore? Even in our earliest days, global threads of influence were being woven into the international tapestry of our homes in New Zealand.

31. *Staff bead as corner stop, initial Busby Residency (Treaty House), Waitangi, of 1833. This ill-related detailing, ineptly using an English interior corner detail, left an unresolved conflict. (Cover boards, fixed later, were removed in a 1989 restoration.)*

32. *Bead-edged corner stop, south wing of Busby Residency, 1842. Round-edged beadings run on 3 by 2 in. (75 by 50 mm) corner stops and weatherboards contribute a "substantial" finish, more akin to 1700s American practice in wood than to English example.*

33. *Wesleyan mission house, Mangungu, Hokianga, 1838. The tallish, gabled dormers with diagonally boarded cheeks bear a strong resemblance to characteristic features of 18th-century houses in Virginia and Georgia.*

Chapter 5

The Fund of Colonial Experience

Learning from the colonies

BEHIND the choice of shape for houses built by Europeans on New Zealand soil stood two to three centuries' experience of the world's hotter climates. Since the early 1500s, adventurous Westerners had been on the move by sea about the world. The superpowers of Portugal (with da Gama) and Spain (with Columbus) led the way. England and France followed a century or more later. All founded trading bases or colonies in the tropical and subtropical belt. All were in contact with native residents, whose established ways of building held many lessons in climate control and economical use of local materials.

The communication of ideas about common people's houses and ways of living, freely crossing national boundaries, is a key theme of this book. We are seeking the ways New Zealand houses were given their forms, and the backgrounds from which our knowledge came. Ideas travelled easily along international sea routes. In placing New Zealand in a latter 18th-century world context, we should not underestimate the amount of sea traffic passing back and forth between countries and colonies around the tropical belt. New Zealand, coming late into this pattern, gained from a global fund of colonial experience. Our house building started from practices learned during two centuries of Britain's seafaring and empire building in many climates, from New England to Virginia and New South Wales, from Bengal to Bermuda, from East India to the West Indies. Available to the early 19th-century settlers, traders, civil administrators and professional army officers was a fund of knowledge shared internationally among colonisers.[1]

34. *Colonial house, Ngaruawahia, Waikato, c 1870. A "feel" of the land and climate lies in these simple elements; but the mix of Georgian trellised posts with naive French-style fringe and French windows suggests more complex colonial sources.*

In the late 1820s, the early houses built by the first independent traders and settlers in the subtropical conditions of Northland's Bay of Islands were probably, for these reasons, a closer response to the New Zealand soil than were the Georgian-styled first mission houses. The settlers adopted from the pool of colonial knowledge such elements as deep verandas, French doors and sweeping tentlike roofs in a direct answer to the climate. Their houses had a simple fitness for their purpose and place, contributing a rightness to their appearance — as was so evident in Gilbert Mair's house at Wahapu.

17

34

14

The veranda

THE veranda has a history in hot lands as old as shelter itself. Its origins and growth as a domestic feature in the Western world are endlessly debated. One probable line of its progress in the western hemisphere started with a West Indies house type of the early 1700s, modified on the American mainland in England's colonies of South Carolina and Virginia by 1740. Well-to-do English planters of tobacco and cotton in

35. *New York Cottage, Throwley, near Faversham, Kent, c 1790. A rare English example of a New York vernacular type, with verandas on three sides, built as a memento by a retiring English army officer after the Revolution.*

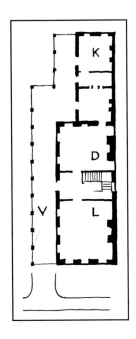

35

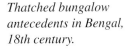

Thatched bungalow antecedents in Bengal, 18th century.

36

THE SCHOOLMASTER'S DWELLING.

Charleston, South Carolina, developed a successful house plan with rooms all in a line for cross ventilation. They apparently derived this layout through trade contact with the sugar-rich West Indies, from an earlier plan which had a roofed porch (locally termed a *piazza*) at each end. But in Charleston they placed a shade veranda on the long side instead, onto which the room doors opened. This simple Charleston plan was the most practical approach in the American South to combating heat and exploiting sea breezes, as judged by Hugh Morrison in his *Early American Architecture*. He also remarked (as noted in Chapter 4) that these stylish Southern colonists kept in close touch with their elite English families. This, it seems, would have ensured knowledge in England post midcentury of their aids to good living. With the beginnings of Romanticism before 1750, and the cult of "the simple life" calling for effective house-to-garden transitions, the attractive Southern veranda must have appealed in England (despite the climate). Its growth there was probably furthered by colonial army officers returning from America after the Revolution.[2]

Another line of the veranda's growth, in England's Picturesque phase (see Chapter 6), came from officers and administrators in retirement from the regular Indian Service after the 1770s, who nostalgically added features from colonial bungalows to their late Georgian houses. The veranda of the Service bungalow, from about 1765 in Bengal, provided a thatched or canvas-roofed shelter round a house core and afforded an enviable level of comfort. A vogue for elegant (but often shallow) verandas arose in England, attached to Regency houses and "ornamented cottages" as well, with exotic additions of Arab or Chinese trelliswork and French doors.[3]

Our word *veranda*, unexpectedly, is not Indian in origin. According to the *Oxford English Dictionary*, it is the Portuguese word *varanda* (railing) taken into Hindi languages as a result of mutual contacts in the 16th century. Verandas were already known in Portugal, and the Portuguese applied their word in India to the lattice-screened porticoes where visitors were received. The word *veranda* was first recorded in English in a 1711 description of an Indian building with such shelters; and the later usage of "verandas" round the Service bungalow became familiar during the British occupation of India. Such was action on the world stage, crossed by colonial travelling players.[4]

36. Cottage Orné, *by J.B. Papworth, in* Rural Residences, *1818. Designed by a noteworthy Cheltenham architect, this extraordinarily fresh concept combines deep, two-storey Southern "living porches" and "oriental" roof forms.*

Caribbean contributions

A further major line of veranda development, again centred on the West Indies, came from French colonial houses of traders, planters and pioneers established from 1700 in the Louisiana territory and in the Caribbean. The principal house type, established on St Domingue (now Haiti) and distributed up the Mississippi valley from about 1735, was distinctive. Round a one-room-deep house core ran fully shaded galleries about 8 ft. (2.5 m) wide, as a "living porch" — apparently an invention of the western hemisphere. A second type was two rooms deep, squarish in plan (sometimes with a central hallway), and with a gabled roof allowing an upper half-storey, with or without dormers. Likenesses — in bell-cast roof lines above surrounding verandas, French windows and planform — are apparent a century later, shared in several of Britain's colonies.

In his *Architecture, Men, Women and Money* of 1985, Roger Kennedy observes that there was "no cottage with veranda in the Western Hemisphere before 1725". By 1750 to 1760, though, they were "everywhere", he says — but only where West Indies traders had reached. The forerunners of the American "sitting porch" thus made virtually simultaneous appearances as a "good idea" around the southeastern states, in a way that cannot be accounted for by normal diffusion. Kennedy states: "No coherent explanation can glue them together except what historians most loathe: coincidence." Acknowledging that these verandas have some parallels in the Indian bungalow, he points out that they nevertheless sprouted in North America wherever sun was hot and rain plentiful, concluding that "the veranda is probably an indigenous American contribution to architectural history". In his *Orders from France* of 1989, Kennedy suggests that George Washington's famed and innovative tall-columned "living porch" of Mount Vernon, added in 1785, was indeed "a two-story adaptation of the 'West Indian' gallery", as seen on his travels.[5]

Among agents transferring house features around the colonial world were professional administrators and military architects who, through their garrison postings, learned practices in America, Jamaica, Egypt, India

Pioneer house on the upper Mississippi, near St Louis, 1737. A St Domingue house, from the French Caribbean, this is one of the first houses with verandas in the Western world. Oldest house in the Midwest, it has a deep-core plan. (Drawing by author based on a photograph.)

37, fig. p. 44

37. *Colonial house, Ngaruawahia, c 1870. The house sits with delightful composure under a single roof line swept over a veranda on three sides, using the simplest of repeated features. The same formula is shared widely, in Sydney as in Quebec.*

Cottage near Renfrew, Ontario, c 1850, its general form showing the influence of nearby French Quebec in its bell-cast roof, veranda on three sides and trellised posts. (Drawing by author based on photographs.)

38

39

40

Pl. 24

and elsewhere. One such architect was John Watts, who served in the West Indies and was then posted to Sydney in 1814. Here he joined Governor Macquarie, himself a passionate builder, who had served in all the colonies mentioned above. The versatility of such men assisted the international spread of proven practices, as well as a uniformity of style, in colonial buildings. Watts' two-storey colonnaded galleries which surround his Observatory Hill hospital of 1815 are virtually the same as those of the Macquarie's Rum Hospital of 1811 (now Parliament and the Mint), slender and gracefully proportioned. The sharing across the colonial world is evident when these buildings are compared with the contemporary colonnaded street of Kingston in Jamaica, and a typical French Louisiana plantation house such as Ormond outside New Orleans, built *c* 1790. A further colonial sharing is evident in the near-universal form of two-storeyed verandas on New Zealand houses.[6]

38. *New South Wales Parliament House (former Rum Hospital), Sydney, 1811.*

39. *Main street in Kingston, Jamaica, 1820. (Painting by James Hakewell.)*

40. *Ormond, a Louisiana plantation house near New Orleans, c 1790: a French-style galleried house of classic proportions with a gently dished roof.*

Rusticated weatherboards

ALSO travelling the colonial world was the imitation of stonework with wooden weatherboarding. In the flat "rusticated board" form, a channel or chamfer was formed at the overlaps, as done in stonework for joints between smooth or rough-faced "rustic" blocks so as to form straight and emphasised joint faces. The first recorded use of the term is by George Washington in 1775, writing about alterations to his house of Mount Vernon in Virginia: "I wish you had done the end of the New Kitchen . . . with rusticated Boards". But the practice itself was older, being used not only on the main house walls in Washington's earlier 1757 alterations, but on several major houses in New England since 1740, notably in the work of **41** Peter Harrison, a gentleman-amateur architect. Broad boards, with chamfered laps hand-wrought by moulding plane, were also grooved vertically to simulate block widths, the whole painted with a sand finish to extend the illusion.[7]

Rusticated boarding appeared in Kent, England, on a few small **42** Georgian houses from 1790. They closely resembled the American examples in board and block proportions, indicating importation of wide boards as well as the idea — which was akin to the imitation of stonework in stucco, Regency-style. The fashion of vertical grooving declined early in 19th-century America, where the boarding continued in its now-customary form, but 13 in. (330 mm) wide. Some rare uses of this plain boarding continued briefly in Kent, but narrower.[8]

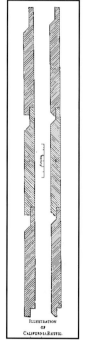

ILLUSTRATION
OF
CALIFORNIA RUSTIC.

In California normal rusticated boarding was in common use by around 1860.

41. *Redwood Library, Newport, Rhode Island, 1748. Rusticated boarding was apparently originated by Peter Harrison, in works such as this superbly detailed imitation of rusticated stonework in grooved wood.*

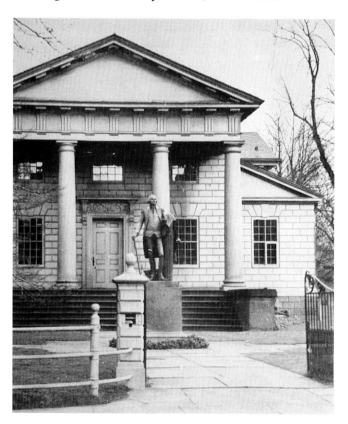

42. *Vicarage, Rolvenden, Kent, c 1810. Rusticated boards are grooved vertically into blocks to disguise this stylish Georgian against the stigma of wood. The window "flat arch" is even grooved with a false keystone.*

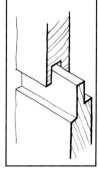

St John's, Te Awamutu: shallow joint profile of rusticated boarding, 1854.

An article on "California Rustic" boarding in *California Architect and Building News* of May 1885, showed typical profiles developed in San Francisco and in universal use there, noting that earlier clapboarding (our tilt-lapped weatherboards) and flush tongue-and-groove were now rarely used. The standard width for "rustic" boards had been reduced from 13 to 10 in. (250 mm) by about 1860. Lap profiles varied from a wide V to a flat recessed channel with splayed lower edge, the commonest form. A channel with curved lower edge was also commonly used.

In precolonial New Zealand, tilt-lapped weatherboards of Kentish late 18th-century type were adopted. But after 1840 rusticated boarding, hand-wrought with a recessed channel joint, was introduced. Examples survive at the The Elms mission house in Tauranga from 1846 (with curved channel foot); on St John's Church at Te Awamutu from 1854 (12 in. (300 mm) boards with tongue-and-groove lap and squared channel foot); and likewise at the Tauranga mission. This shallow profile continued into the 1870s in the main cities, but was superseded by the simpler halved lap and deeper channel type of San Francisco form, in 10 in. (250 mm) boards.

43. *Rusticated boarding in local redwood at Mendocino, North California, shows the curved channel profile as used in New Zealand.*

43

44. *Houses in the Vieux Carre, New Orleans, 1780s–1850s. Paired cottages show their connections with French sugar colonies of the West Indies in shuttered French windows, bell-cast* **37** *roofs and peaked dormers.*

French windows

SIDE-HUNG sashes in pairs opening inwards had been the standard window of continental Europe since the early 1700s — that is, about the time the English were replacing their traditional hinged casements with the new Dutch-type "double-hung" windows. Simple pairs of narrow, glazed windows, known to us as French doors, give a familiar and distinctively New Zealand character to our earliest houses. Their transfer here from New South Wales, or directly from Regency England, was but the last step in their progression through the fund of colonial experience. From late Georgian Picturesque cottages they can be traced back to Caribbean

44 island French colonies and to houses of New Orleans in the 1700s, there combined with outward-opening airy louvres. But the innovation of opening rooms directly to the outdoors through "French" doors came ultimately from the Versailles of Louis XIV in the 1680s. There his architect Hardouin-Mansart designed the Grand Trianon as a "retreat" palace, having its major rooms located unusually at ground level with easy access to a garden terrace — through windows taken down to the floor.

Chapter 6

First Imports:
Revival of History

Early settler houses, 1820–1860

HAVING now met up with members of our "house family" in various parts of the world in the 18th and early 19th centuries — and some of their ancestors — we may more easily recognise their progeny in this land in the early years of settlement.

In our precolonial days, as we have seen, much house design depended indirectly on the worldwide funds of folk and colonial forms. From many sources, distinctive types of houses had been developed in the British and French colonies, which combined indigenous forms (such as the Bengali "bungalow") with devices common to the tropical zone in general (such as verandas and sunscreen grillages). The British "colonial house" appears strongly on the scene in the first wave of New Zealand houses built in our precolonial period by worldly traders and missionaries in the north. **Pl. 9** It was brought by them not as a Colonial Service house (as it was to the New South Wales colony) but more through their familiarity with the tropical types, or with stylised versions of such houses which were currently popular in parts of Britain. It was not a house for the common man in early 19th-century England, but more an elite fashion that disregarded the English climate.

To these earliest settlers we ultimately owe our familiar four-square, hip-roofed cottage of the later colonial decades — usually with a front veranda the full width of its "double pile" plan. With two rooms on each side down a central hallway, this freestanding one-storeyed house was a model for many of our 1840s houses, and introduced the form that would

45. *Church House, Cookham, Berkshire, mid-19th century. This sharp, almost strident expression of the "picturesque" Gothic image was spread by numerous plan books from English and American sources.*

endure as the core of undoubtedly the commonest New Zealand house type into late Victorian times.

It is striking that, once raw pioneering exigencies had been dealt with, the kinds of English house types adopted in New Zealand were markedly selective. The localised Kentish Georgian rural houses may well have provided our wooden building techniques and an initial style, but this adoption probably stemmed more from knowing a serviceable building technique than from pursuing a sentiment for "home". Subsequently, design of houses seems to have been more influenced by the current style in Britain, despite New Zealand's remoteness, than by any sentimental wish by emigrants to reproduce the homes they had left behind. England's move **45** into Gothic Revival style, steep-roofed and angular, soon influenced the form of many houses in our early settlements of the 1840s. But little attempt was made here to recreate, for instance, the stone, gabled forms of central Cotswolds cottages, except indirectly within Gothic Revival's vocabulary of forms. Likewise, some resemblances to Scottish crofters' huts occur in South Island cob or stone cottages; but they are as likely to be the result of universal folk-form forces — which can produce a similar rectangular hut anywhere given comparable conditions — as of the urge to recreate a remembered home. Instances of such earth or stone cottages in New Zealand are fairly rare: they did not become typical, common houses.

Contrary to the traditional pattern of colonists' building efforts, therefore, little attempt seems to have been made by our specific immigrant groups to reproduce closely the types and forms of their houses from "home". Neither industrial row houses nor cottages becoming rural slums held an appeal as models, any more than did the ubiquitous brick terraced houses. We might note that these normal British houses "remained basically unchanged throughout the [Victorian] period", as Marshall and Willox commented in *The Victorian House* (1986), "apart from superficially different decorative embellishments". In contrast, it is of interest that New Zealand's common houses varied greatly in a succession of styles, and were subject to change and development throughout the same period.

63, 69

Early house style

BY the 1850s, then, the typical houses being built in New Zealand showed little nostalgia for the earlier forms of "home" in the "old country". Here, the Kent and Sussex weatherboarded manner gained stylish verandas and French windows. There, its Georgian rural style remained, not much touched by the newer Gothic or Italianate fashions of midcentury. However, in New Zealand the Kentish weatherboarding tradition was soon adapted with ease to clothing these new styles.

Clearly, our early settlers looked to the latest Gothic Revival or Italianate manner popular in Britain at the time, rather than the style of the traditional British homes they had known. Their attention seemed to be firmly on the present and the promise of the future, with little desire to dwell on the past they had thankfully escaped.

Consciously raising their individuality above the level of basic shelter, many of New Zealand's early houses were up to date and "stylish" from the start — more than might be expected for first settlements on remote and little-known islands. A degree of sophistication — or at least

46. *Duncan Cameron's house (St. Keven's), Onehunga, c 1847. Conservative persistence of Regency detailing is seen in this large version of the square, peak-roofed colonial house.*

of awareness and enterprise — was evident. Numerous individual settlers, including resourceful professionals conducting official duties, enterprising traders and merchants, and missionaries with airs and ambitions, introduced different plan forms and design ideas. Some built their houses by drawing on their own skilled experience, a few imported precut frames knocked down, while others had houses built according to their own ideas or chosen models.

Gilbert Mair's orderly trading establishment with his handsome house at Wahapu in the 1820s has already been described. The Waimate North mission houses of the early 1830s were larger, using a rural Georgian core plus colonial verandas. Both Duncan Cameron's house (St Keven's) at Onehunga and Hulme Court in Auckland adopted, in the 1840s, a hipped, symmetrical block surrounded by refined Regency veranda detailing in trellis-panelled double posts and slender, curved brackets.

Judge Martin's informal house of the early 1840s in Parnell, shipped out from England, had a faintly Regency air with its three higher room units linked by lower rooms, all as standard "modules" neatly fitted together. In Thorndon, Wellington, at the same time, chief surveyor S.C. Brees illustrated one-and-a-half-storeyed Gothic Revival houses, with a steep-gabled, strong-roofed L shape and a wraparound veranda.[1]

At Hurworth in the early 1850s, near New Plymouth, Harry Atkinson built a small, finely proportioned farmhouse, with its side entry against a massive central chimney block between two rooms — the compact, traditional English "lobby-entry" plan (as adopted and perfected in the New England colonies). With gable eaves projected in the "bracketed mode",

14
13
46

47. Harry Atkinson's house (Hurworth), near New Plymouth, 1855. Both main rooms are provided with generous French windows onto a **47** *surrounding gallery of West Indies type, in an appealingly direct design.*

and fully encircled by a veranda, all its features show awareness of the "Swiss cottage" style then in vogue.[2]

The presence of such houses set an appreciable standard towards which ordinary settlers might look. Initially, their simple houses adapted local means to ends, in the universal geometries of folk buildings. These included the expected one- and two-roomed huts, plain equivalents of rustic cottages in England, now timber framed and weatherboarded. But some sense of style and pride brushed off on the common man's idea of his house: by the 1860s the new towns exhibited a range of house shapes that expressed more than just utilitarian pioneer shelter.

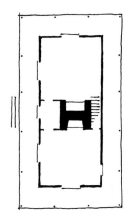

Plan of Hurworth.

Early house shapes

THE primary folk-type basic house form was the "rectangular cabin" (*A*), often modified to a T shape by means of a gabled roof across one end, projected as far as the veranda edge (*B*). The rectangular unit itself could be doubled across the rear under a lean-to roof, or else under a second gabled roof with a valley gutter.

In larger schemes cross-gable roofs were placed at both ends of the rectangular unit, in a broad H plan (*C*). In one-and-a-half- or two-storeyed forms of the same plans, upstairs bedrooms were either part attic or full-height spaces. Even an Italianate tower might be attempted at the front door or in the corner of the veranda. Grander one-and-a-half- and two-storeyed houses, with doubled cross gables flanking two storeys of verandas, were also seen.

After the rectangular cabin, our second major basic house form — the deep, squarish plan (*D*), with a fully hipped roof, and a veranda across the front or around three sides — was somewhat less flexible by nature of its centralised form. Nevertheless, variations were played in dormers to attic rooms, and changes of scale were telling, culminating in large, two-storeyed blocks with spacious veranda galleries around several sides.

At the other end of the scale, as the larger towns became more crowded and land more tightly subdivided, the basic rectangular, gabled cabin was turned end-on to the street. The characteristic "shoebox" houses were the result, in one- or two-storeyed narrow blocks with windows and doors only at their ends, placed close together (but not joined).

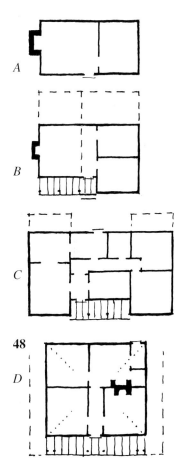

Classical and Romantic: 18th-century Britain

IN opening Chapter 2, I said that architecture in the latter three-quarters of the 18th century in Britain was dominated by the classical spirit of Imperial Rome, as interpreted in the Georgian style. This simple statement sufficed to keep our directions clear on the founding of the Australian colony. But, of course, reality is never so simple. The picture needs to be filled out a little.

On one hand, the classical "villa" returned to the scene in England

48. *A range of narrow-frontage "shoebox" cottages in Elizabeth Street, Wellington, c 1890.*

during this period, for the first time since the end of the Roman occupation. Through the early to middle 1700s, architects Colen Campbell and the true amateur Lord Burlington led a group of arbiters of taste in a revival of the design principles of the great Italian architect Palladio. His **49** classic villas and palaces, built some 150 years earlier, were seen as supremely harmonious compositions in the landscape of the Veneto. Rigorously symmetrical, with a columned "temple" portico flanked by wings of greater or lesser extent, they made noble the rustic grandeur found in traditional Italian farm complexes. The concept of the formal villa exemplified the ideals of the English Palladians: the villa, standing free in its own grounds, was presented as the correct and desirable residence for a man of quality and taste. As built by Campbell and Burlington himself, the villa thus entered the Englishman's psyche; and in ever-diminishing scale, from country house to small detached house in town, it has remained high among his aspirations ever since.

On the other hand, within this suave and disciplined period of Georgian and Classical persuasion, seeds of other ideas were germinating. As always, certain creative minds were disposed to explore beyond the *status quo*, unconfined by current dictates of style in their search for fresh paths of expression. In reaction to both the austerities of Classical logic and the extravagant artificiality of society life at court, a countermovement in Europe began seeking a new naturalness and simplicity. Initially in a somewhat wistful manner (the court ladies at Versailles, dressed as

49. *Villa Capra (architect: Palladio), near Vicenza, northern Italy, 1566. An extraordinary and influential Classical masterpiece of impeccable harmony and "presence".*

milkmaids, played in make-believe farm buildings), the quest for "the simple life" gained strength by midcentury. Largely due to the genius of Rousseau in his discourses on natural man, a profound shift in attitude and human feeling occurred. With a changed understanding and virtual worship of Nature, man saw mountains and brooks with a fresh sensibility, and his relation to the outdoors altered. Goethe chose to live in a small cottage in a garden. To feel at one with nature . . . Sir Kenneth Clark, in *Civilisation* (1969), clearly expressed the aim: "to lose our identity in the whole and gain thereby a more intense consciousness of being".[3]

This underlying current of the cult of nature (and of its cousin, the Picturesque) would emerge fully, later in the 18th century, in the Romantic movement in all the arts. Its consequences eventually affected every aspect of the 19th century's character — including typical New Zealand houses from the first decades of settlement onwards.

To perceive what had been happening behind the placid Georgian style of our colonial houses, we need to look at some of the agents of change that had been at work in the 18th-century world. We have already noted influences deriving from the fund of colonial experience. As well, in a paradoxical duality through most of the century, the enlightened and rational Georgian Age was at the same time admitting its very opposite, a pursuit of the picturesque and irrational, of quaintness and irregularity. A taste for exotic novelties (fed by the exploration of foreign lands) was indulged, along with imitation "gothick" fantasies in garden structures and ornamented cottages. The erection of follies, some in the form of ruins, added piquancy to the landscape. The Picturesque manner was so named to express those "painterly" qualities by which buildings were indistinctly blended in a landscape, evoking a mood of the past as found in the landscape paintings of Claude and Poussin.[4]

In the 1760s a darker side was seen in Walpole's *The Castle of Otranto*, the first Gothic horror novel; and Walpole himself had the interior of his large house redecorated with richly traceried surfaces of "gothic" inspiration. His use of such forms was more vigorous and charming than the customary lifeless applications at that time; but it was a purely decorative surface, lacking the constructional logic of true Gothic works. From that point revival of the Gothic style gained pace as a fashion. A strange

50

50. *Endsleigh (architect: J. Wyatville), Devon, 1810. A* Picturesque *cottage orné. Not lacking in artifice and exaggeration, this early example of the Romantic retreat is displayed as the setting for an ideal "natural" life.*

51. *Royal Pavilion (architect: J. Nash), Brighton, Sussex, 1815–1821. Seen from the approach side the exotic palace is the ultimate fantasy of minaret airshafts and pleasure domes.*

mixing of gothic ornament on classical houses appeared in the latter Georgian age.

From around the 1750s the Picturesque brought together several streams of antirational ideas and sentiment. Based in Romanticism and with "the natural" as its guide, it turned a sharpened eye to the charms of the visible surroundings. The "picturesque" was sought widely, specialising in the eccentric, the exotic, the whimsical and the evocative. Delight was found in ornamented forms from any source: the quaint spell of Gothic, intricate fancies of Arabia and the Near East, foreign flavours of distant China.

51

Anachronistic though it may seem to us, and with overly sweet affectations, the Gothic style with its steep roofs and high-pointed, filigreed gables soon prevailed. The flippant "wedding-cake" and "gingerbread" connotations should not deflect our attention, however, from the vigorous intent that was growing in the movement of ideas at that time. What had emerged by the middle of the 18th century as an occasional taste for the exotic became, by the early 19th century, a liberal and strong framework of radical thought. Romanticism challenged established canons of "correct" formal design, and opened the way for admission of an alternative, assertively "natural", voice. The results were mixed: on one hand, artificialities of the Regency period were discredited; but on the other, the belief was growing that any style of the past could be revived — a mind trap that persisted through the century, offering a plethora of options among "styles".

In the event, the pragmatic and self-confident bases of the 19th century's industrial advances were opposed by the Romantics' ideals and their retreat from reality to the past. The whole period was marked by opposites, a stream of vocal campaigners polarising social and aesthetic attitudes at all levels. The plight of the working masses was set against benefits from the industrial revolution; handcrafts and the dignity of work were contrasted with the brutalising effects of industrial production; and a yearning for the medieval life of chivalry and pageant opposed the world of steam, science and steel.

All these issues were unleashed within the intricacies, strengths and contradictions of Victorian thought and life. The revolution in taste which accompanied the start of the Victorian Age also penetrated other

56

52. The Gables (architect: F. Thatcher), New Plymouth, 1847. A former hospital. With its framework structure decoratively exposed, this Gothic Revival essay was up to date with English fashion.

countries in Europe and America, and came with the immigrants to New Zealand. Despite the remoteness of colonial New Zealand, the country was caught up in the fervour from the very start of the Victorian era. Although "official" building initially kept to the calm, hip-roofed, colonial Regency manner, buildings designed for other purposes — such as churches and schools — frequently show a pseudomedieval character deliberately sought in their exposed heavy-carpentry frames, steep roofs, diamond-leaded panes and carved details.

Gothic Revival forms, brought to this country by architects in the early 1840s, soon appeared commonly on houses in Wellington and Nelson particularly. The firm repose and horizontal lines of the late Georgian style were being replaced by stressed verticals, asymmetrical forms, 60-degree gabled roofs with tense angles, and filigree ornamentation on roof verges. To our eyes they look old — certainly old-fashioned for their time — and somewhat quaint in feeling. Yet in reality they were up to date with the latest international style, then developing in England. It was in fact the quietly simple, elegant and (to us today) fresh-looking late Georgian buildings that were out of date and old-fashioned.

53. Hawkstone Street, Wellington. Latest-style houses by mid-1840s. The one in front is not "pioneering" — forked branches as posts were a popular Picturesque device in England. The Gothic-style cottage behind is asymmetrical, with carved bargeboards and apex finials. (Detail, engraving after S.C. Brees, Pictorial Illustrations of New Zealand, 1847.)

The entry of the gardeners

DESIGN of the independent house in its country setting was a central issue of the Picturesque movement in England. From the time William Kent (1685–1748) first created the English landscape garden around 1730, the assertive presence of the country house was gradually muted to become part of a total landscape instead of its focus. Kent saw all nature as a garden and was among the first advocates of naturalism in landscaping. To this end a certain irregularity in house forms was encouraged. In the later 1700s this quality of diversity was applied to decorative, rustic cottages on private estates, usually built as garden ornaments but at times inhabited. For these romantic accents in the landscape the Gothic style was favoured, with its evocative associations and natural blending of material textures.

It was another landscape designer, Humphry Repton (1752–1818), whose many works gave visible form to the new belief in nature and the ideal of the simple life. His concept was that of living within a natural landscape: not simply of seeing it as a "picture" from inside the house, but of linking the interior of the house inseparably to its surroundings. The connection of house to grounds was altered by placing formal terraces, lawns and flower gardens close at hand, as transitions to the naturalised park beyond. In his work around the early 1800s, he considered the design of the house to be of equal importance to his "landscape gardening" — his own term — in a planned concept of indoor–outdoor connections. Instead of being raised on the traditional elevated base, the main floor was lowered to be level with the ground or terraces, and links to the garden were made practicable by verandas and balconies. Repton himself wrote of the idea "borrowed from the French, of folding glass doors opening into the garden", producing an effect "like that of a tent or marquee".

The concept of the new approach was thus established in Regency England. But as D. Pilcher pointed out in *The Regency Style, 1800–1830*, the provisions of verandas, French windows and living rooms level with terraces were not introduced for their practical advantages so much as for their role in conveying a romantic view of architecture and the qualities of the picturesque. Getting closer to nature was the aim. The garden was even brought indoors with flower stands, trellises and vines adorning walls and ceilings, while arbours, aviaries and conservatories later became incorporated in the house itself.[5]

Repton expressed the ultimate ideal as "camping" in the landscape: the house as an elaboration of the tent. The sense of impermanence conveyed in this Romantic view was indeed a characteristic of much Regency Picturesque design. (Loosely termed, the Regency style covered several refined fashions under the Prince Regent's regime *c* 1810–1830.)

The literal idea of "tent-like house" made elegant contributions to the shaping of a number of small houses in England and of innumerable houses in the colonies. The connection with Britain's colonial experience cannot be overlooked, especially in the Indian Service's familiarity with permanently canvas-roofed houses of considerable comfort, their side walls in

54. *Graceful profile of the small New Zealand colonial cottage — two rooms deep, hipped shingle roof, rusticated weatherboards and awning-like veranda — here retaining Regency wrought-iron filigree ornamentation. Wanganui, c 1880.*

part draped out as awnings. The effect was sought in the design of Regency verandas and porches, roofed balconies and even — in a festive air — of main roofs gracefully curving up to a central peak. A slightly dished curve was adopted for verandas on delicate iron frameworks, their sheet-metal roof panels painted in alternate bands of colour like striped awnings. And here is the image of one of the most charming early New Zealand house types — that peaked, squarish cottage wrapped by verandas under sweeping roof lines, which we have already encountered in early Northland. As well, we recognise our Victorians' persistence in painting the corrugated-iron sheets on their veranda roofs in alternating bands of white and red or green: the marquee concept died hard!

54

Only the wealthier in Britain could indulge their pursuit of the "natural" and "picturesque" life, as advocated by Repton and architects with their pattern-book "ornamented cottages" — those charming gatehouses, caretakers' lodges, quaint summerhouses and similar dilettante extravagances for their estates. In the last of the Georgian years, however, development of the modest freestanding house in the countryside was promoted by the influential books of John C. Loudon (1783–1843) — also a landscape gardener, and an experienced agriculturist. His volumes in the 1820s dealt in turn with gardening, agriculture and plants; and in 1833 his vast *Encyclopaedia of Cottage, Farm and Villa Architecture and Furniture* covered not only everything for the farm but also an array of **55** remarkable proposals for houses in rural settings. These house types ranged from farm labourers' cottages and sensible paired dwellings (early semi-detacheds), through Anglo-Italian villas and German-Swiss chalets, to an Indian-Gothic domed lodge — as well as small, battlemented cottages and other whims and absurdities. Along with many other pattern-book designs of the period, Loudon's styles reveal an eclecticism based on sentiment, guided by little principle other than pursuit of the individual and "picturesque" that was unleashed by the Romantic spirit of the times. More down to earth than most, however, Loudon advanced practical ideals of country living and landscape qualities to a wider audience.

55. *A selection of Picturesque cottages from* Loudon's Encyclopaedia of Cottage, Farm and Villa Architecture, *1833: many-chimneyed Rural, arcaded Italianate, and pointed Gothic.*

In the 1840s — the decade of New Zealand's founding as a British colony — yet another significant landscape gardener and author, Andrew J. Downing (1815–1852), entered the scene, this time in the eastern United States. He espoused with enthusiasm the rural Picturesque manner of Repton's English landscape gardens and the range of cottage homes illustrated by Loudon and other English advocates. Downing transported the principles and ideas to America and popularised them through his books. He set out to define ideal kinds of small, inexpensive but characterful houses suited to independent American families, all to be freestanding and built on their own plot of land in town suburbs. In several enormously influential books, two of which went into many editions, he promoted a series of thoroughly considered designs of cottages with "feeling", and of modest country houses for the average man. Steep-roofed English Gothic with ornamented gable verges, or lower-pitched Italian modes with bracketed eaves — both were handled with convincing common sense and imagination, with little idiosyncrasy. Indeed their conservative floor plans often have a central entry or a gable on a symmetrical frontage, instead of the romantic eccentricities prevalent in English examples. He gave practical advice on enhancing a house by careful planning of site relations and plantings, as well as detailed discussion of purposes in house planning — in many ways close to a modern popular architectural approach.

Many of the house designs themselves were by Downing's friend, Alexander J. Davis (1803–1892), an outstandingly talented architect. He was a very early entrant in Gothic Revival works in America and enjoyed a lengthy and prolific career. The stylish panache was Davis's; the easy and persuasive words Downing's. Significantly, they introduced all-wooden houses into the Picturesque scheme of things, albeit at first with some diffidence, and by the 1850s their designs and recommendations were a clear foretaste of the later American "frame" house, standing free on its generous lot at the edge of town. The charisma and influence of this interlocked pair of A.J.D.s was immense. Downing is seen by many American authorities as the chief progenitor of the American suburb's charac-

56. *Rustic Cottage, 1837. A.J. Davis's seminal design which spawned a stream of American Gothic Revival houses in wood, promoted by Downing's books. Vertical board-and-batten style seen on 1840s New Zealand walls may originate in Davis's houses and churches.*

ter, advocating independent houses on their gardened plots in a spacious setting, in contrast to the ills of the congested city.[6]

American Gothic Revival houses

AT an early stage, A.J. Davis had in 1836 made a design for a steeply gabled gatehouse, to be clad in vertical boards with the joints covered by projecting wooden battens — the first architect to apply this boarding to houses. He soon used it in a "rustic" Gothic cottage design with steep roofs, pierced wave-line gable verges, elaborate chimneytops and a bay window, which he published in his *Rural Residences* portfolios from 1837. This Rustic Cottage not only became the basis for several cottages propagated by Downing's books: it also established the quintessentials of the Gothic Revival house in the United States for the next 20 years. With vertical board-and-batten sheathing stressing the verticality of its stance,

56

57. *Gothic Revival house, Queen Street, Thames, Coromandel, c 1870. The steep-roofed style leads to one-and-a-half-storey layouts. Waveline and carved bargeboards join with "gothic"-patterned veranda brackets.*

58. *Highwic (initial cottage portion), Epsom, Auckland, 1861. In spite of its apparently English airs, Highwic is one of numerous houses directly inspired by American Gothic Revival designs during the 1860s in New Zealand.*

57

(Below left) Design **58** *VII from Downing's* The Architecture of Country Houses *(1850).*

59. *(below right) Cottage Lawn (architect: A.J. Davis), Oneida, New York, 1849. The same elements and* **60** *proportions as at Te Makiri, 17 years later, are evident.*

the distinctive theme was quickly taken up throughout America — and in New Zealand.

Picturesque Gothic Revival houses were plentiful in our early towns of the 1840s and 50s, mostly built in wood and many clad with vertical boards and battens very similar to those detailed in Downing's examples. That Downing's books were known in New Zealand is evident. Indeed, the initial core house of Highwic, dating from 1861 at Epsom in Auckland — the ornamented residence of a wealthy businessman, and an icon of early New Zealand houses — has been traced back to Downing's Symmetrical Cottage (Design VII in *The Architecture of Country Houses* of 1850, the floor plan of which fits even to the door and window locations), together with parts of Davis's influential Rustic Cottage design of 1837 (the pierced gable verge is identical). Bearing equally unmistakable similarities in form and plan to Downing–Davis models is Te Makiri in Helensville, built in 1866. In this case, a blending is apparent of Design VII (as at Highwic) with the farmhouse Design IV and cottage Design II in Downing's Cottage Residences of 1842. Very strong resemblances also

60. *Te Makiri, Helensville, of 1866, shows remarkable parallels to Downing and Davis designs, and to Cottage Lawn (see 59) in particular. The oddly broad bargeboards suggest replacements, awaiting restoration of the gable fretwork.*

exist with Davis's Cottage Lawn house, built in 1849 at Oneida, New York.[7]   **59**

Only by coincidence did Joseph Burnett adopt the name Oneida for his remarkable Gothic Revival house built in 1869 near Wanganui. (Of Scottish descent, he had lived in Oneida County, New York, during the 1830s.) Local architect George Frederic Allen produced an extraordinary design, evidently inspired by deep feeling for American Gothic-style   **62, Pl. 10** houses and Burnett's shared interest. Although clearly conversant with Downing–Davis practices and details, Allen's design yet appears to be unique. New Zealand's finest wooden Gothic-styled house, Oneida, in its imaginative boldness, is fully equal to any American original.[8]

Some of the appeal of Gothic Revival houses to New Zealand settlers may have been in their familiar, perhaps comforting, "Englishness" in an unfamiliar land, as well as in their being fashionably up-to-date. It is ironic   **61** that the best of our Carpenter's Gothic should be so American in source.

61. *Gothic Revival house, Mission Street, Santa Cruz, South California, c 1870s. The Downing–Davis type-form of Highwic, seen at home in exotic surroundings: American formal symmetry prevails.*

62. *Oneida (architect: G.F. Allen), Fordell, near Wanganui, 1869. A dynamic and original New Zealand composition, in full American Gothic Revival style. Oneida's soaring rooftops house an inner hall 45 ft. high (13.7 m).*

Towards the suburban life

IN one further aspect, Downing's successful books have a characteristically American stamp. Plan books and advisory design manuals emanating from midcentury America often contain moralising sentiments on the social value of the individual private home. To Downing, the caring tastes which embellished a home were an "unfailing barrier against vice, immorality and bad habits". And its Gothic-style forms, true to tradition, were associated with elevated Christian thoughts. The proper family values nurtured there were the foundation of a stable democratic society. Moreover, a love of beautiful forms and an appreciation of the charm of "the tasteful cottage or villa [with its] well designed and neatly kept garden" were encouraged "for their pure moral tendency", as "an outward expression of inward good". The virtues of home ownership were extolled as a way to strengthen the individual's social role with stability, a worthy figure being the industrious workman whose house stood on the ground he owned.

In promoting these views, Downing was in fact renewing ideals expressed by early founding fathers of America. William Penn, English Quaker, in planning the new Philadelphia in the 1680s, wanted an open-spaced town with every dwelling in the centre of its plot. (Prosperity and urban congestion saw to it otherwise.) A century later, Thomas Jefferson aimed for an egalitarian sharing of the nation's land, among independent citizen–farmers in a democratic state, each with a house on his own piece of land. From Jefferson and Downing onward it has been the domestic ideal of America — indeed, one expression of the American Dream — for every family to own a plot of land with their house on it. The faith has been reaffirmed constantly: by poet Walt Whitman in words, as by Frank Lloyd Wright in architectural vision through his 1930s Broadacre City project, a Jeffersonian anti-urban concept with its citizen–farmers residing on one-acre plots.

Ownership of the family home has today become a hallmark of the middle class, and a detached house in the suburbs remains an ideal held dear across the United States. Alexander Downing's aim was the betterment of the houses of his countrymen as "a powerful means of civilisation", and as an ideal for the republic's good. He helped mould the suburb to the status of a new norm, to support and protect the healthy family life of the common American. Further popularising of the suburban home in similar terms was undertaken by Catherine Beecher, an early champion of recognition for women as "the professionals" in charge of the domestic workplace. In the 1840s and 50s both Downing's and Beecher's proposals and ideas were promoted by small builders and popularised through the pages of women's magazines.[9]

In the middle of the 19th century this suburban condition was novel in several respects: the rapid growth of railway services (and later, tramways) made it possible for business people and other city workers to distance their homes from the noisesome industrialised centres; land on the outskirts was plentiful, hence its economical subdivision could be more generous in area; and so the freestanding house, with all the family liberties it promised, could at last become a dominant residential form. (To place these 1840s American developments in a wider historical context, it is well to note that the singular St John's Wood suburb of superior semi-detached houses in London was only just under way; that a further 30 years would elapse before the relatively dense Bedford Park suburb was built within Chelsea; and that another quarter-century would pass before the Garden Suburb movement gained an effective place in Britain.)

Meanwhile, in 1840s New Zealand, hasty actions were taken to sub-

68

divide land in towns under Gibbon Wakefield's theory of colonisation, with the planned provision of one-acre lots. The intentions were significant, if not radical. Although his social planning of land ownership proved too simplified, the subdivision plans had at least predisposed emigrant settlers towards the freestanding single-family house on an ample lot. This ideal, cherished by the New World, was attainable by settlers here almost as a matter of course on the uncrowded land. From early years, too, individuality in the appearance of houses was sought, in the Picturesque manner; and this goal of "difference" was to persist thereafter in a full Victorian assertion of individualism. The die was cast early for New Zealand's eventual open and varied housing patterns, in country, town and suburb.

In the American industrial cities of the Victorian period, living conditions differed little from those in their British counterparts, notorious for their squalor, degradation, congestion, disease and exploitation. By the 1850s, prosperity and immigration to the States had led also to urban concentrations there, and terraced or row housing based on English prototypes was adopted everywhere in the eastern cities. We will return to the British inner-city house forms later in this chapter; at this point, though, it is of interest to compare the attitudes towards suburban living and home ownership in Britain and the United States in the second half of the 19th

63. *Terraced houses, Ashton Old Road, Manchester, 1860. Early Victorian restraint and some finesse mark this otherwise standard example of British housing for the common man.*

century. The lofty ideals for the suburb as promoted by the American
house reformers have been outlined above; the British approach was more
pragmatic, driven by a simple urge to escape.

By about 1870 horse trams enabled British clerks and other lower-
middle-class workers to avoid the debased housing among the factories
and to reach the first belt of crowded suburbs. In later decades of the
century, mass transport by railway allowed the working classes to reach
the outer suburbs as well. They occupied speculatively built rows of
attached dwellings, near standard in plan. For the better-off among the
middle class, the choice of a more exclusive suburb at a greater distance
from the city centre was wider, offering a higher standard of row house
and semidetached — or even, for the fortunate, a small villa.

63

In the Victorian code, to live well removed from one's place of work
was a sign of respectability. Marshall and Willox in their book *The
Victorian House* (1986) interpret the wish of the English "to be able to
close their front door on the noxious city when their work was done" as a
definition of the Victorian home. Home was a bulwark against the outside
world, which was shut out by the house door — a genteel haven in which
to escape from the noise, dirt, smells and crowded commerce of the
industrial-age city. It sustained an inward-turned lifestyle, provided the
safe refuge so favoured by the English, as alluded to in Sir Edward Coke's
words of 1644: "for a man's house is his castle". But, as we shall see, this
assertion applied more to a man's private freedom indoors than to his
ownership of property.[10]

There is little echo here of the American idealists' suburban community of neighbours, where Downing's "smiling lawns and tasteful
cottages" proved that a civilised "order and culture are established". The

64. *A suburban street at
Kennebunk, Maine, in 1950,
illustrates the continuous
front lawns, classic porches
and immense trees of the
American domestic ideal.*

64 characteristic open front lawns of the American suburb, unfenced and with great trees, appear from this time as the public setting of the free-standing home: the private space for garden produce and family activities is found in the board-fenced back yards.

The ideal of the independent citizen's ownership of his own home is itself in marked contrast in the two countries. In the United States, although reality fell short of the ideal, a census of 1890 showed that nearly 40 per cent of American families nationwide owned their own home, a figure likely to grow with the general increase in the population's wealth. In comparison, only some 10 per cent of British Victorians owned their own house, the normal practice being to rent dwelling units in speculative housing. Home ownership as a dominant aim does not seem to have been characteristic of the British at any time.

On the other hand, "two main features of the New Zealand housing scene", according to the *New Zealand Official Yearbook* for 1990, are the single family's detached suburban house, which "has been the predominant type of dwelling in New Zealand since European settlement", and "the preponderance of owner–occupier tenure". Home ownership figures from the 1916 census (the first to have covered the matter in New Zealand) indicate that 52 per cent of dwellings and flats were owned by the occupants, with or without mortgage. Clearly, ownership of one's own home has been at the root of ideals of independence shared by the "new" societies of New Zealand and the United States. Also significant is that the 1916 census showed just under 97 per cent of New Zealand dwellings were separate, the acceptance of semidetached houses and flats being minimal.[11]

Home in the neighbourhood

FOR whatever reasons and causes we may determine, the way New Zealanders have thought of home and neighbourhood, in their suburban or semirural surroundings, has been far closer to American ideals than to British customs. The conventional New Zealand pursuit of the privately owned freestanding house on its own land has produced patterns on the landscape of similar density and scale to those of many United States suburbs and country towns. The model of the worthy man achieving independence by owning his home on its garden site has been in the American Dream since the early days of the nation: we have seen it repeated across three centuries by Penn, Jefferson, Downing, Whitman and Wright. Even the New Zealand Company's settlements, under the influence of Wakefield's theories, can be seen to approach this general spirit — at least for those having "sufficient" means. In 19th-century New Zealand the opportunity to achieve "rugged self-reliance" in the yeoman tradition may also have played a part in freeholders' owning and cultivating small holdings. A similar attitude among town dwellers may have valued the security and independence of home ownership (or at least a mortgage contract).

Our survey has raised some of the ideas prevalent in the world of New Zealand's early settlers and administrators touching on their view of their homes. It is striking that so large a part was played by landscape gardeners. Clearly theirs was no peripheral role: their specific interests and skills were the catalyst in the physical achievement of the Romantic movement's ideals. Through a 100-year span they led the growth of a new feeling towards the house in a natural environment. That it was not "just the same as before" is borne out by recent research which dates the innovation of the informal flower garden, planted in beds, to be as recent as 1735. And to dispel the thought that Victorian landscape gardeners may have been impractical dreamers, it is well to recall that it was one of them, Joseph Paxton, who created the 1851 Crystal Palace — a triumph of advanced techniques using iron and glass in mass-produced units on an unprecedented scale.[12]

Out of this background of romanticism conflicting with industrial progress, New Zealand acquired much of the new "naturalist" attitude at a critical time: it appears to have been directly relevant to our early settlers' conditions, hopes and opportunities. Granted, it was more often beds of cabbages and potatoes than flowers that adorned the settler's front garden. But once through our pioneering phase, the ideal of the freestanding house in its "natural" garden flourished, not only characterising that most widespread of Kiwi living patterns — a love of the outdoors and the tending of private gardens — but also conveying the most cherished image of "home" in New Zealand. Nevertheless, that image seems to have been coloured by the generous scale and flavour of America's spacious suburbs for the common man.

In early Victorian Britain, Picturesque naturalism had not been available to all. Ornamented cottages and artful Gothic retreats were originated for the pleasure of the affluent as decorative accessories on their estates, not for the common man residing in towns. But the style did move into the public eye on the occasional parsonage (a significant if modest form of freestanding family house, with strong Victorian associations). In particular, it was adopted widely for certain toll houses, railway houses

65

65. *"Home" in New Zealand, pioneer style:*
45   *a love of the outdoors and the care of private gardens continue the Picturesque tradition here.*

66. *Railway stationmaster's house near Southwell, Nottinghamshire, c 1850. Charming in the Picturesque Gothic manner, like a gatekeeper's lodge, but oddly incongruous with the rapid machines it served.*

66 and small station buildings. (In a typical Victorian paradox, the most modern transportation advance since the invention of the wheel was often given a medieval setting.) There was little or no chance, however, that everyman might acquire an independent freestanding house on the outskirts of Britain's cities and towns: his dreams remained confined to the long rows of continuous house buildings and tenements for the duration of the century.

53   But in New Zealand, the small-scale Picturesque cottage provided a model to emulate for an outdoor lifestyle in the mild climate of the new country. What was more, the common man could hope to enjoy its pleasures. Given New Zealand's plentiful land, he was able to acquire his own home on his own patch with an ease he could not have expected

67. *An early bungalow's living porch, c 1920. The easy indoor–outdoor connection of the "picturesque" house in its New Zealand setting — in a relaxed and unaffected style.*

under Britain's established housing practices. The Picturesque house thus became a practical addition to the range of developed house types known to the settlers, from among which they might choose.

Meanwhile, in Britain a prospect for the future had, however, been ventured. Around the beginning of the 1800s a radical housing layout had been proposed for a new suburb at St John's Wood, then lying at London's edge adjoining Regent's Park. Instead of terraced housing, paired houses of moderate size were to be built, divided by party walls along their boundary line, thus presenting buildings of substantial scale as well as a sweep of garden embracing each house on three sides. Development did not commence until the 1830s, and then in greatly modified form; but the revolutionary intent of building a suburb mainly of semi-detached houses was pursued. The blend of urban and country living appealed to many among the prospering middle class. The two-storeyed houses were kept close to the street, on lots with a frontage of some 35 to 40 ft. (10 to 12 m) for each unit and about 150 ft. (46 m) deep. Surrounded by trees and privacy (as they still are) the houses must have presented a concept of "home" approaching the ideal.

This was the first part of any town, in Sir John Summerson's words, "to abandon the terrace house for the semi-detached villa — a revolution of striking significance and far-reaching effect". As conceived initially, in 1794, this unorthodox scheme preceded the Garden Suburb movement by nearly a century while introducing similar elements.[13]

Victorian housing

IN the midcentury Britain from which most of our settlers came, the social and urban changes after 75 years of accelerating industrial revolution were profound. The convergence on main cities of the interdependent new systems — of transport, steam power, factory production, labour and commerce — was forcing vast urban growth, with great pressure on existing social establishments. The social structure itself had already been changed by the steady rise of an educated and influential middle class — a stratum, that is, between the landowners and the labourers. This growing layer of city-based merchants, tradesmen, businessmen and professionals, moreover, had money to spend on buildings. Proliferation of the painted-stucco, classical terraces of Belgravia was one outcome; fine public buildings to house new institutions were another. A third was the housing built for throngs of workmen drawn to the cities on whose labour the new enterprises depended.

To house the massive population increase, the classic terraced house was reduced and debased for the common man's dwelling in the city. The flood of people from the country exchanged their cottages — often little more than rural slums by today's standards of "home" — for terraced urban slums. The old villages had been built with cottages abutting each other in continuous rows: the same convention produced monotonous row housing for the working populace in the cities, with brutalising effect. Other than the rare philanthropist, nobody paid serious attention to the housing needs of the ordinary man.[14]

The factory, with its polluted environment and devouring economy, dominated everything. As there was no public transport, dense housing areas were built within walking distance of workplaces. Living conditions, in the belt of grimy Midlands towns, the Potteries and London, dropped to one of the lowest ebbs since civilisation began, as the mortality rate bore witness. New social problems inevitably arose everywhere as Britain's population increased fourfold between 1800 and 1900.

Not all housing for "the masses" at this time descended to the degraded level of the notorious "back-to-backs", however (and, over time, major social reforms were initiated on an unprecedented scale, along with **69**   a vigorous religious revival). Terraces of two- or three-storeyed row houses of reasonable quality were built, whether by factory owners, landlords or the multitude of speculative builders, to cater for the innumerable social strata from labourer to clerk to tradesman. Much of this housing stock, constructed almost invariably of brick, remains lived in today. House de- **70**   sign was largely a matter of enrichment by degrees, on unchanging plan layouts; and every element or decorative device on the row-house terrace or the semidetached was class conscious. The convenient, endlessly repeating floor plan itself had in fact been standardised before 1700. Nikolaus Pevsner described it in his *Outline of European Architecture*: "With its entrance on one side, leading straight to the staircase, one large front room

69. *Terraced houses, Ashton Old Road, Manchester, 1898. Perennial Victorian housing. Design was static across 40 years, but coarser in detail since the prior example illustrated (63). (The window sashes are modern.)*

70. *Terraced house details, Beaumont Road, Bournville, Birmingham, 1905. Class definition by ornament: a gable, and faintly Ruskinian Gothic arches and bay, distinguish this repeating unit of a standard terrace (see* **Pl. 1***).*

and one large back room on each floor . . . it remained practically unaltered for the largest and smallest house until the end of the Victorian period." (Inevitably, it was also a basis for Victorian two-storeyed house planning in New Zealand — and in America as well.)

The pressures of overcrowding in the main centres remained relentless. It is small wonder, as John Gloag noted in *Men and Buildings* (1949) that the country cottage "has, since the early nineteenth century, had a profoundly sentimental appeal for the English householder". But equally unrelenting in 19th-century Britain were rules of class which decreed the type of house a family might occupy: row houses in the city or close suburbs for the working class; terraced houses of better quality, or rare semidetached houses in outer suburbs, for the middle class; freestanding houses only for the privileged — and well spaced in the better outer suburbs. In the country, with the economic degradation of village life, the farm labourer's lot was seldom more than a hovel.[15]

New Zealand emigrants

IT was to escape the worst of those 19th-century social and physical conditions that most free-passage emigrants to New Zealand chose to leave Britain. Would they have wished to recreate the squalid housing of the Victorian cities in their new land, or the crumbling medieval cottage rows of a depressed countryside? If they took with them any images of their ideal home in the promised land, they are more likely to have aimed to emulate the newer types of houses seen on the outskirts of English towns.

In his book *Georgian London* (1945), John Summerson reviews the city's outward spread at the end of his chosen period, at about the time of Victoria's accession and her acquisition of New Zealand. He lists several types of fringe development, from the true suburb enjoyed by prosperous middle-class merchants living in trim stucco villas or brick country houses in nearby old villages, to occasional modest detached houses among streets of terraces and groups of cottages on the traffic routes out of town. Small as well as large, late Regency villa or early Gothic Revival "ornamental cottage", it was probably houses such as these that stirred the emigrants' aspirations. The significant factor is that their aim was for separate, free-standing houses.

From the beginning, the ideal of equality has coloured the New Zealand way at every social level. In Victorian England, though, the free-standing house was rarely the home of the common man; this was the preserve of the privileged. Could our immigrants now, in their new land, claim their liberty from privilege?

The revival of history

ALREADY by the mid-1840s, as we have seen, intentionally old-fashioned English Gothic-styled houses, of Picturesque irregularity, had **52, 53** been introduced to the New Zealand settlements. They joined the mix of house types gradually evolving here out of the fading classical Georgian– **71** Regency styles, which were themselves shifting towards the bolder Italianate character. Indeed, for the next 50 years in New Zealand both the Italianate and Gothic styles would be pursued through their many fashions, in parallel and even combined.

In England, from around 1830 and during the first years of the young Victoria's reign, the Regency style, which John Nash and the Prince Regent commanded for decades, had been losing its vitality and was increasingly the subject of criticism. It was not only under scornful moral attack by supporters of Augustus Welby Pugin in his effective crusade for a return to the "true principles of pointed architecture" of Gothic England. There was also unease caused by Nash's last Regent's Park terraces, where skin-deep painted stucco covered many constructional sins and equally shallow design. The strengths of restraint exemplified by the Georgian terraced houses had weakened. Regency charm and elegance verged on the effete, and the light touch of playfulness had too often **51** become licence. The audience was getting bored with the superficiality, the deceptions and the shams.

In the middle of this period, the 1830s, 24-year-old Augustus Welby Pugin (1812–1852), in his pamphlet *Contrasts*, launched his shattering criticisms of the superficiality and vulgarity of so much that passed for contemporary design. He condemned the use of Gothic shapes simply for their decorative appeal and for evocative associations alone. His lessons brought about a new sense of respect for the constructional principles which underlay all the forms and ornament of true Gothic buildings. His effective propaganda and later example did much to set the Gothic

71. *Detached house in St John's Wood Terrace, London, c 1850. This small-scaled house makes full use of a range of Italianate elements in stucco.*

Revival on a serious footing of proper research. As well, he forged an earnest moral link between a religious life and architecture — a portent of the Victorian age's sterner side.

Nevertheless, in the growing ferment of Victorian ideas, not all were convinced by Pugin's arguments for a return to Gothic 13th-century ways and forms, even if the "foreign" borrowings from pagan Classical architecture were to be replaced by a return to sound English Christian practices from her past. It was argued that Classical values were by then an integral part of the British mind and systems, so the images associated with them were also seen as an appropriate architectural expression. Division between the opposing camps persisted for decades in the so-called Battle of the Styles. *Both* factions developed their causes with strength, from broad intellectual foundations, resulting in a fascinatingly rich invention of vigorous forms and bold concepts.

Romanticising of the medieval past tends to obscure the fact that the latterly named "gothic" (i.e. barbarian) methods of building had no such nickname in their own time. In reality they were the product of a clear-headed, brilliant age of scientific skills and invention taken to the limits. Their boldly rational cathedral structures were as "modern" as they dared to go in exploiting the physics of forces applied to materials, typifying their period in the way that passenger aircraft of today typify ours. But by early Victorian times, three centuries of Classical revivals had demoted the Gothic to a romantic "style", decorative, complex and "mystical" in character.

Architects of classical persuasion in Britain continued their chosen tradition with strengthened principles, in a more "correct" pursuit of Classic and Renaissance example. Works of power and scholarly richness confirmed their stance. As time passed, lines of allegiance to the two opposing factions became blurred by a general eclecticism, which allowed a free choice in styles.

Victorian attitudes

Do not fail to speak scornfully of the Victorian age: there will be a time for meekness when you try to better it.

J.M. Barrie

THE dependence on historical styles by Victorian architects in the clothing of new buildings — which, as some would see it, condoned the pillaging of past eras — should not too quickly be attributed to poverty of originality or imagination. The Victorians, as we well know, were of a highly inventive turn of mind. They were curious about their world, avid for knowledge and self-improvement, and dedicated lecture-goers: their support for Athenaeum, Mechanics' Institute and public library speaks for itself. An enthusiasm for things historical engaged their minds, in a period marked by widening research into prehistory and evolutionary theory. Contributing to the architects' absorption with past styles would have been the exciting finds unearthed by the archaeologists of the time. Their astonishing coups, from Delphi and Nineveh around 1840 to Mycenae and Luxor about 40 years on, fired the public's imagination with forms from the distant past.

72. *Main platforms, Central Station, York, 1871. Both sides of the Victorian coin: exciting, sculptural interior spaces, in dynamic structures of steel technology and machine-production — but supported on cast-iron columns with Roman designs.*

Artists responded with epic-scale historical paintings of exotic events, and with evocative images of life in past times. Alma-Tadema displayed his "noble" fantasies of Roman luxury; Rossetti wrote poems and painted his "blessed damozels" in a dream world, yearning for the truthful medieval days; Burne-Jones depicted languorous beauties of vaguely Arthurian times. Such images reflected the architects' dilemma of choice between Classical and Gothic — the Battle of the Styles. Melodrama and grand opera epitomised Victorian popular sentiment.

Architects' versions of borrowed historical features would have appealed to the educated middle classes caught up in the popularity of the historical novel since Sir Walter Scott's day. Later, Lord Tennyson's "Idylls of the King" — a middle-class favourite — confirmed the thread of romanticism running through the whole period.

Alongside their respect for history and historicism the Victorians were also fascinated by the achievements of new technology, mass production **72** among them. The deep conflict felt to exist between machine industry and humanist values both characterised and bedevilled the whole era. From Pugin and Ruskin to William Morris, strong minds were set against the tide of rationalism and the machine. But their passion to return to medieval practices was too idealised and was to prove futile against the powers of "progress" and mass production.

Romanticism, the new worship of Nature, and a yearning for medieval times: all were given form in the buildings of the Gothic Revival. At the same time that the industrial revolution was thundering on towards the future, many thinkers and most artists and designers were longing to go back into the past. In a word, the Victorian paradox.

The architects saw their work as a culmination of all that had been achieved before, so they aimed to build on the past, with intelligence and assurance. Indeed, many of the leading architects were very well informed and confidently proficient in applying a wide range of historical styles. Nevertheless, some of them (including the High Victorian Gothic master, Butterfield) felt reservations of conscience over the lack of true creativity in their work. But they could not see that it was their fixation on the necessity to apply a style of ornamentation that was itself the barrier. Not until the early 20th century would some release be found, in the functionalists' belief in the rightness of structures built without ornament at all.

"Behind the facade of confidence," wrote P. Skipwith in *Apollo* magazine (April 1992), "the nineteenth century was increasingly a period of doubt; it was an age that did not know itself, and turned hungrily to the ancient world to try and understand its own psyche."

Chapter 7

Pacific Neighbours

Eyes on California

AUCKLAND and Wellington are years older than the town of San Francisco. When the new settlements at Auckland and Wellington were alive with construction activity in the early 1840s, both San Francisco and Los Angeles were no more than small Mexican villages beside old Spanish forts. They lay quietly on a remote fringe of the American West Coast, which Spain had counted as hers for more than two centuries. Wellington's population by 1843 was about 6,000, Auckland's about 3,000: San Francisco had around 500 people.

Since 1770 a number of Franciscan missions to the Indians had been established at intervals up the 500 miles (800 km) of coast north of Mexico's border. California settlers and ranchers enjoyed a relaxed existence, centred on the provincial capital of Monterey. A number of Yankees from the East acquired huge cattle ranches on the coastal fringe in the 1830s. From the 1820s New England whalers (then also frequenting New Zealand shores) built whaling stations up the California coast, and Yankee traders were also dealing in hides. American interest was mounting.

Following a sporadic war with Mexico, the United States in 1848 annexed a vast territory from the Californian coast across to Texas, and in 1850 California was made a State in the Union. In the meantime, gold had been found in 1848 in the Sierra foothills, and the first rush came with the "forty-niners" in the following year. San Francisco's future was transformed: her population rose in two years from about 800 to 25,000. In a decade the westward migration of the American peoples, by sea and land, was boosted by 100,000 adventurers of no fixed abode — who were about to become New Zealand's new neighbours.

The initial annexation of the Californian lands in 1848 was more of a political and territorial "positioning" for the future than a migratory process. But the discovery of gold at the moment of annexation precipitated the San Francisco coast into becoming the ultimate "western frontier". Leapfrogging from the previous frontier of westward expansion — which lay at midcentury a little to the west of the Mississippi River — this new coastal frontier had no supporting hinterland. Only the most tenuous routes connected it by land to the rest of the United States. The immediate dependence of California on routes by sea was underlined by the 500 deserted ships which shortly jammed the shoreline of young San Francisco. (Abandoned in the rush to the goldfields, they were used as makeshift accommodation before being buried by urgent reclamations for city land.)

Though now part of the Union, the state of California could hardly have been more remote. Inland from the coast to the previous frontier of settlement (that is, to the Missouri and the great Mississippi Valley), stretched a wild 2000-mile (3200 km) route through rocky mountains, waterless deserts and great plains: two-thirds of the American continent to cross, on the risky California and old Oregon trails. The normal line of supply from the Atlantic coast cities, by clipper around the Horn to San Francisco, was a stupendous 16,000 miles (almost 26,000 km). (It was only 13,750 miles (22,140 km) from New Zealand via the Horn to England.)

In the other direction from San Francisco, however, southwest by sea, the pocket of Western civilisation in New Zealand lay only 7,000 miles (11,250 km) away. (It was 800 miles (1300 km) further to reach the colony of New South Wales direct.) No wonder, then, that little time was lost in developing trade between Auckland and San Francisco from 1849.

Dozens of small sailing ships had been built in northern New Zealand during the 1830s, largely by Maori taught by white settlers, and they were busily trading around the Pacific by the late 1840s, including to the American West Coast and even China. By 1850 Maori farmers were achieving a surplus production of wheat and other produce from their tribal cultivations and sought a larger market overseas. Through the 1850s, therefore, local and overseas ships became engaged in carrying New Zealand cargoes of wheat, potatoes, salted butter, pork and beef to the teeming Californian goldfields.

Food supply took a leading role. For two or three years from 1849, flour grown and milled on John Morgan's mission wheatfields at Te Awamutu by Waikato Maori raised high prices on the California goldfields. John Logan Campbell (later called Father of Auckland) took a shipment of potatoes, onions and other produce to San Francisco in 1850 at a huge profit. Robert Graham, pioneer farmer at Ellerslie and later developer of thermal resorts, shipped potatoes and wheat to California from 1850 to 1853 as well as trying his fortune on the goldfields. And Samuel Revans, journalist and importer, went with a cargo of timber and potatoes in 1851, in partnership with prominent merchant Nathaniel Levin.[1]

In 1849 a young Thomas Macky, emigrating from Londonderry

during the potato famine, joined his brother James' wholesale firm in Auckland. As a venture, they had 20 portable houses prefabricated in kauri timber — "very neat little cottages" — and shipped them in late 1849 to San Francisco, along with a large quantity of groceries, timber, bricks and other goods. Given California's isolation the houses were expected to sell for five times their cost; but, by the time of their arrival, "immense quantities of timber coming round from the Eastern States" caused a loss, the sale of all 20 recovering the costs of only three. But the potatoes, onions, oats, sugar, candles and wine sold well.[2]

It was in such ways as these that New Zealand kept in touch with the West Coast of America's fortunes and development. Of course, gold itself also stimulated considerable movement of people from New Zealand to the Californian fields in the 1850s and, in the return direction, to the later gold strikes in Australia and then on to the South Island of New Zealand during the 1860s. Trade and contacts between San Francisco and the South Pacific, including New Zealand, increased from 1860 following the Australian gold discoveries. (Mark Twain visited New Zealand from San Francisco in the 1860s.)

California's connections to the rest of America improved only slowly. It was not until 1858 that coaches operated on the Overland Stage Route to the east, and it was 1860 by the time the famous Pony Express provided the first quick (10 days) communications link between California and the interior at the Missouri River. The first telegraph line was connected in 1861; and it was a further eight years, marked by Indian hostilities, before the saga of the Pacific Railroad joined the East to the West with a major transport service, at Sacramento in 1869. (Los Angeles, far to the south, then numbered only 6,000 people.)

It was in 1870 that a significant link between New Zealand and San Francisco was established with the initiation of a regular mail and passenger shipping service. Using steamships contracted by the New Zealand and New South Wales governments, the San Francisco Mail ran four-weekly from Sydney and Auckland via Honolulu. The journey from Auckland usually took about four weeks. The new transcontinental railway also meant that a much faster route from New Zealand to England was now available, across the States and by ship over the Atlantic from New York. By 1880 the journey took six or seven weeks in all. A fresh and close awareness of the New World was opened up to travellers from New Zealand. A stream of information and influence from the vigorous American West now flowed along the communication links with California, which were much shorter than those with the "old country".

By 1870 San Francisco had become a major metropolis. The city's character was ebullient and showy, its life patterns original and extravagant, its buildings mostly brash and ostentatious. Greater settlement of the fertile inner valleys of California soon followed appraisal of the state's many resources. By no means backward, indigenous Spanish-Mexicans maintained an agreeable life on their ranches. The wealthy Vallejo family's 1856 house in Sonoma was an up-to-the-minute, Gothic Revival, post-Downing design with lacy bargeboards and fretworked veranda. In many other ways Eastern Yankees made important contributions to early Californian development. Their inventiveness, shown in hydraulic-sluice gold-mining methods, water races and quartz stampers, was also felt in many other construction fields, including the logging industry. (Indeed, their technical skills were carried to New Zealand goldfields and forests as well.) Mariano Vallejo himself sized up their inventiveness: "The Yankees are a wonderful people: if they emigrated to Hell itself they would soon manage to change the climate."[3]

During the 1860s and 70s the new Californians set about developing their distinctive housing styles, remote from the taste-setters of the East Coast. By 1880 San Francisco's population was 250,000 — equal to half that of New Zealand.

Style in the American East

IN order to understand our Californian neighbours' fresh kinds of houses and their potential significance for New Zealand, we need to consider briefly the established styles of architecture in the Eastern states. The architects there looked to England and Europe for guidance and standards in design — after all, the historical styles they were applying to their buildings came from those sources in the first place. For a few decades after the War of Independence in the previous century, there had been a temporary — but understandable — turning away from the inherited English styles based on Wren and Gibbs towards, first, French and, later, Greek alternatives. However, interest in English ideas was renewed in the 1830s, and the Gothic Revival was embraced warmly across America, reshaping houses as well as public buildings. Its advocates, Pugin and Ruskin, were read widely; and works by leading English architects, such as Gilbert Scott and Butterfield, became influential among American architects, largely by way of the English journals. The Classical School, as well, continued in force with works by Nash, Barry and Cockerell contributing to American versions of the Renaissance or Italianate styles, which also affected domestic architecture.

Architects in the Eastern cities, in designing houses for a small elite group of clients, built mainly in stone or brick after the manner of their European historical style models. But away from the dense cities and among lower-income levels — in areas scarcely touched by architects — timber was the widely used material for house building. This major practice was not transferred from Europe, but had long been indigenous to America's common houses because of the nation's huge forest resources.

For the broad field of popular house building, from the 1850s certain American architects and building draftsmen translated European style models from stone or brick construction into forms suitable for local construction in wood. Everything — from the main walls, their openings and surrounds, columns and cornices, porticos, brackets and pilasters, to fashionable decorative details — took on new proportions and a new character. Designers of pattern books in the northeastern states, usually architects, extracted key features from styles and modified them in a

Popular American design for a farmhouse (or a suburban cottage), c 1870, typical in the Eastern to Midwestern states: a "frame" house with Gothic-style porch and Italianate windows translated into wood construction — and a multicoloured, Gothic-patterned roof.

distinctive American vocabulary of design which exploited the techniques of execution in wood.

Promoted by plan-book guides, therefore, the Gothic Revival and Italianate styles were being popularised in wooden construction on everyday houses for the common man across the country. The development of wood-based decorative and fashionable styles proliferated at all social levels. Local woodworking mills, making increasing use of steam-driven machinery, entered production of pattern-book components — doors, windows, mouldings and turnings, decorative fretwork in brackets and panels, staircase balustrades and so on — thus expanding the available design vocabulary into a house style for the community. Occasionally even basic "folk" houses were raised above plainness by fitting them out with stock items, copied from fashionable houses seen locally: a moulded door surround here, fretsawn veranda brackets there, and a piece of gable "drapery" elsewhere. Scroll cutting, using improved mechanical saws, became a popular outlet for limitless invention and occasionally naive expression. In *The American House*, Mary Foley remarked that "with the help of the new American scroll-saw the costly stonework which distinguished Gothic Revival mansions soon was translated into wood. The result was the Victorian 'gingerbread' house." The word

73. *American Italianate house style, from E.C. Hussey's plan book* National Cottage Architecture, *1874. This familiar-looking design, with the masonry Italianate style's features, was intended for wood frame and boarding.*

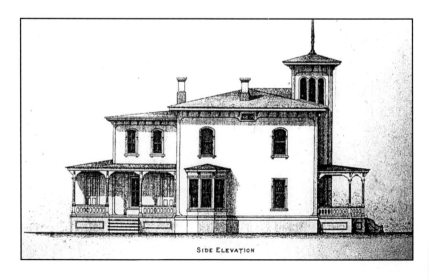

SIDE ELEVATION

gingerbread — oddly, an old English term for gaudy decorations on ships — was given new currency in American usage.

Alongside the Gothic Revival, the style called Italianate was devised in England in the early 1800s, conveying a picturesque and romantic image of vaguely irregular walls and distant towers, placed in an idyllic, classical landscape and redolent of Italian rural life. John Nash appears to have been its originator in 1802 with a country house near Shrewsbury named Cronkhill, a stuccoed, asymmetrical composition of two storeys in which he used smooth, strong forms deriving from rural Italian villas, plus the wide eaves of southern farmhouses, mainly for pictorial effect. He extended this visual eclecticism in detached groups at the Regent's Park Villages built in the late 1820s. John Loudon followed, applying the manner to some of his cottage and villa designs in his *Encyclopaedia* of **55** 1833. The style in general embraced loggias with round-headed arcades, a square tower off centre with "campanile" arches under a low, peaked roof, irregular wall heights, low-pitched gables and broad, flat eaves on **68, 73** multiple brackets, and grouped windows with arched heads. A small, glassy, belvedere turret sometimes capped the roof. The English bay window, as ever, soon took its place in the picture, although it was scarce in Italy.

From the 1840s onwards the Italianate style dominated in the United States through the middle decades of the century, based initially on the English works of Nash and Charles Barry. In the Eastern states, A.J. Downing's widely read plan books of the 1840s and 50s extolled the "Italian" style's virtues alongside the "Gothic". With A.J. Davis's design assistance Downing promoted in particular the "bracketed mode" with wide eaves, which he found highly suitable in the American climate for its sheltering and richly domestic character. The role to be played by a variety of shaped wooden brackets under roof edges is explained in his *Cottage Residences* as "giving a character of lightness" to a villa. This was an early exposition of the vital part that decorative brackets were to play in the growth of the style thereafter. The Italianate style was spread widely by pattern books, among which *Villas and Cottages* of 1857 by Calvert Vaux (an expatriate English architect and, briefly, a partner of Downing's) was very influential across America. A major presence of the American Italianate style was in city row houses after the 1840s, among which New York's "brownstones" would be the most famous.

US styles, Western-style

THE more urbane East Coast set the standard for American sophisticated design, in the fashionable English and French house styles. The indigenous American wooden versions differed considerably from each other from one state to another, and nowhere more so than in California. It suited San Francisco's buoyant mood to display a wealth of ornament **74** and, frankly, wealth itself. Elaboration came to be piled on elaboration in an orgy of extravagance.

Little seems to be known about the builders of the city's houses in the 1860–1880s period (many official records were lost in the 1906 earth-

74. *Italianate twins in California Street, San Francisco, c 1875. Lavishly ornamented in carved and moulded wood, this pair expresses the self-confidence of early San Francisco.*

quake and fire), and minimal influence by architects is apparent. Showing remarkable inventiveness, newly arrived carpenters, builder–draftsmen and designer–builders with a good eye seem to have answered the optimistic mood with a rich array of motifs. In a decade or two San Francisco had its own distinctive style: the builders, working alongside joinery shops and millwork suppliers, developed their themes practically anonymously, taking liberties in wood with the East Coast's Italianate style extended to its limits. Inevitably the audacious results were regarded with disdain by architects and arbiters of taste in the East.

Academic knowledge of architecture was not needed to join in this joyful and creative work, adapting older forms to new combinations: voluptuous, double-storeyed bay windows, elaborately carved porches, and everywhere those radiant, disproportionately high cornices crowning the houses like florid Victorian hats. Gothic Revival was renewed with a vertical élan in the ribbed repetition of members on the wooden surfaces, oddly incorporating Classical motifs in the mix as well. San Francisco's Victorian style was an extrovert phenomenon of popular culture — in its origins, in its assertive development, and in its expressiveness. Not reserved for a wealthy elite alone, the machine-made flourishes were available for all: flamboyant, sensuously rich to the eye, an outward declaration of good fortune.

By the 1870s, then, a free variety of the American Italianate style was being applied with enthusiasm, skill and consistency to produce the city's vertical and spectacular wooden houses, standing tautly in close-packed ranks on the narrowly subdivided land. From the start, uncontrolled land speculators had divided the limited buildable land into narrow plots. In

75

the 1860s many wooden houses were simple single-storey dwellings of four rooms, but the predominant type of two-storeyed, narrow, upright house was already established. A range of typical floor plans was devised, several of them peculiar to San Francisco, to meet needs brought about by dense occupation of the hilly site. Typical subdivisions had lot widths from 18 ft. (5.5 m), on which fully abutting two-storey row houses were built in the inner city, up to 35 ft. (10.5 m) for freestanding houses in zones further out. All were around 90 ft. (27.5 m) deep.

In the Western Addition district from the 1870s on, the common lot size was 25 ft. by 100 ft. (7.5 m by 30.5 m), for which a standard row house type was planned, with a recess about a metre wide (called a slot) running halfway down one side, where a dining room projection closed it. This separation let light and air into the deep house plan. Wooden buildings had been banned after 1853 in a 30-block area of the central city, but they were favoured elsewhere for their dry and healthy conditions, safety in earthquakes, low cost and easy ornamentation. Very large numbers of them, to the west and south of the central area, survived the 1906 disaster.[4]

Lying across San Francisco Bay from the city, the East Bay towns had their own character. Among them, Oakland had been everyone's starting point for the transcontinental rail journey across America after 1870. Here the houses were rather more down-to-earth but nonetheless advanced in style. San Francisco's crowded and hilly subdivisions (as in Wellington) had limited the range of house types, but sites in Oakland, Berkeley and Alameda were initially rural and level, giving free scope for a greater diversity. We shall return later to these towns of the East Bay.

By the 1870s the San Francisco region's wealth had stabilised, with the more orderly mining of Nevada silver in place of the golden chimera, and the city grew, aided by world trade, into the main port on the Pacific coast. Rapid development of towns and industries occurred along the coast,

75. Houses in McAllister Street, near Alamo Square, San Francisco, late 1880s. Paired individualists in current Stick–Eastlake style (see pages 135–6), intricately ornamented and bound together in a tense, vertical rhythm along the street.

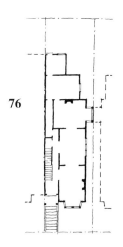

76

Standard San Francisco Victorian row-house unit, main floor plan. A blank party wall and a projecting bay combine in an effective, dense plan.

76. *House in Golden Gate Avenue, San Francisco, c 1890. Emphatically wooden in Stick–Eastlake style with slightly splayed bay, and separation "slot" for side light and air. Their colour contrasts earned such houses the name "painted ladies" even in 1885.*

centred on the earlier mission settlements, and in the fertile valleys of the interior to the east and north of the city. A huge timber industry and its supporting towns flourished in the north of the state around the prodigious redwood forests. The radical method of economical timber construction called balloon-framing (on account of its lightness) had been invented in Chicago around 1840. Initially using slender studs of two-storey height, it was later developed on the Coast into Western "platform framing" in which only one storey height at a time was erected. It made possible the rapid growth of the Californian towns, and the Coast's abundant fir and redwood timbers, easily cut and nailed, met the need for speed. Speed, too, was the magic of the new American woodworking machines which, with their versatility, soon encouraged extremes in the profligate use of ornamental members.

Life on the frontier

BY this point interesting parallels can be seen between the circumstances in which Californians and New Zealanders found themselves in the second part of the 19th century. Let us start with the fact that both these emerging communities began, within 10 years of each other, with a pioneering stage on relatively virgin land at two of the outer limits of Western civilisation — California at the farthest western frontier, New Zealand at a virtual frontier on the farthest land east before the change of

77. *Napa Valley, north of San Francisco. A New Zealand landscape in California. Lush pasture, low metal barns, wire fences, pockets of trees on softly rounded foothills, and dark-clad ranges behind — all add to a feeling of* déjà vu.

day. Between the two lay 7,000 miles (11,250 km) of Pacific Ocean. Their main population centres, San Francisco and Auckland, lay at exactly the same distance respectively above and below the equator.

The two communities therefore shared a similar temperate climate, and they spoke much the same language. They also shared many of the "frontier" characteristics which play a consistent part in forming the attitudes of such communities. In both countries, a new social group was finding itself and creating its internal bonds. Both also faced resistance by indigenous peoples.

77

The defining qualities of frontier societies, and their significance to American life, were first clearly propounded by Professor Frederick Turner at the end of last century, in papers published as *The Frontier in American History* in 1920. Many processes he describes are directly comparable to those experienced in the early development of New Zealand, where social and economic growth apparently followed patterns typical of a frontier society. Three fundamentals of such societies are seen as: first, the physical tasks of clearing the land for agrarian use; second, the problem of credit finance for farm development, usually becoming a debt burden in depressed times; third, the search for markets for production surpluses. In dealing with these problems certain trends are emphasised, bound up with survival of the community: a leaning towards egalitarian attitudes within a social democracy, the placing of a premium on physical and moral virtues, the discounting of social standing through birth or even financial status, and pressures to conform with community work ethics. All of these attitudes gave a particular tone and character to American frontier life, and had parallels in the New Zealand experience. In expectation of change, an openness of mind was connected with the idea of "progress". Frontier communities optimistically adopted policies of inflationist financing, borrowing to build roads and railways and for general development, and accepting a level of continuing debt — a clear parallel to the Vogel government policies of the 1870s in New Zealand.[5]

The westward movement of its peoples has been a constant in United States (and world) history. Pioneering groups of settlers have progressively moved further westward, and their independent thinking and adaptation to new lands have challenged the national establishments in the East. This important factor has contributed to the growth of the American national character and its assertion of democratic ideals. The frontier process has repeatedly promoted institutions and customs it values and abandoned others that have lost their meaning. The result has led towards direct populist government by wide representation, and against class rule; to freer opportunities for all; and to a new status for women, which recognises gender interdependence. Frontier life, facing risks and danger, ultimately becomes idealistic.[6]

These conditions of frontier life seem familiar steps along the path of New Zealand's 19th-century development. The finding of common ground between New Zealand and California occurred naturally from our initial trading contacts with San Francisco in the 1850s. Given the "frontier spirit" felt by many of our immigrants who left Britain in order to better themselves in a new, free world, stories recounting the vigour and successes of US settlers in California must have been reassuring. Overlaying sentiments towards their original "home", an attractive alternative model was offered, of a different but relevant kind: the American West showed a way of *opportunity* ahead.

Finding house-building ways in common

THE similarity of conditions on East Pacific and South Pacific shores — social, climatic, geographical, historical and material — presented many opportunities for exchange of views, methods and eventually products in the field of house building. The abundance of high-quality timber resources for all general building needs was a major ground for sharing ideas and techniques. New Zealand imports of American building materials, tools, hardware and joinery products were considerable by the 1860s. It is likely that interest extended to their methods of house construction from this time, not only through our similar framing and weatherboarding inheritance, but also through practices related to a timber-based house-building economy and to low-density residential land use in general — in neither of which areas did British precedents offer guidance.

Pl. 11 The gold- and silver-mining towns of the American West, from California to Colorado, may well have contributed some of their building methods and styles to New Zealand through the 1860s' gold rush to the South Island fields. The mining towns in both countries certainly shared marked likenesses in their "instant" wooden buildings — including those square-topped false fronts raised to mask a sloping roof behind. Knowledge of the new American balloon-frame methods of light-timber construction, including Western platform framing, is likely to have come with the miners and their followers. These techniques, replacing traditional tenoned framing with all-nailed "four by two" construction, were adopted as the normal method of building the New Zealand house by the 1880s.[7]

A lasting thread of general influence is also likely to derive from later activities of the "thousands of diggers [who] remained in the country as permanent settlers" (as stated in the *Descriptive Atlas of New Zealand* of 1959) after coming from the United States and Australian goldfields. Among them or their associates would have been tradesmen with skills needed on the mining sites, including carpenters and surveyors (who may have spread American practices in house building and land subdivision). Certainly knowledge of advanced timber structures was introduced, with American technology in hydraulic gold-mining and logging operations, as evidenced by the impressive trestle-framed water flumes (aqueducts) to feed sluices in the South, and major log-driving dams in the North.[8]

By 1870 New Zealand's house-building activity was reflecting signs of material improvement in the common people's condition. More than 80 per cent of all dwellings were now built in wood (according to the 1871 census, and excluding Maori housing) and less than 3 per cent in brick or stone. The remaining 17 per cent included huts and small dwellings in cob, sod, raupo reeds or canvas. On average there were a little under four rooms and six occupants per dwelling.

As Ngaio Marsh observed, writing of the expatriates' condition in *An Encyclopaedia of New Zealand* (1966): "It is inevitable in a community that has come into being through a tough unremitting struggle with the land itself that the emphasis should be on material gains and on visible, useful, and tangible development." Visible expressions of material gains were now occasionally seen in "stylish" changes on the simpler houses — a trend towards greater flourishes in the outlines and piercings of veranda brackets, more complex profiles of wooden brackets under the eaves, and more intricate fretwork attached both to gable ends and bay windows. Enrichment of one's own home by a few touches of exterior ornamental display gave tangible proof to all and sundry of one's personal achievement.

By this time New Zealanders were probably familiar with American fashions in dress and furnishings, and with some aspects of popular house styles. In *Wise's 1883–84 Directory* importers advertised the latest goods, from guns to house furniture, with American sources ranking equally with British and Continental suppliers. The growing level of New Zealand's business links with San Francisco is indicated by a two-page article in the November 1883 issue of *California Architect and Building News*, previewing "a massive six-story building of pressed and enameled brick, Oamaru free stone, and California granite" to be erected on California Street for the New Zealand Insurance Company.[9, 10]

Wooden enrichments

DESIGNING and making ornaments of many kinds in fret-sawn, scroll-sawn, moulded or turned wood was now universal in the United States. Scroll work had become a form of popular art, with a national flavour of its own, from fret-sawn picture frames on the wall to gingerbread scroll-work from stem to stern on Mississippi steamboats. The variety of bracket patterns was endless: some were derived from plentiful Victorian books of artistic designs and a few from architectural plan books, but many more

78

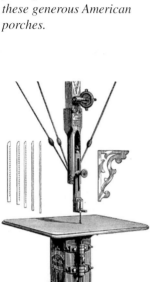

were worked out by local timber mills for themselves. In the US John Maas wrote, in his book *The Gingerbread Age*: "Gingerbread is part of the universal design language of the nineteenth century. The very same scrolls and curlicues are found in Victorian ironwork, in the patterns for Victorian needlework . . . and in Victorian printers' fancy typography . . . Houses aren't built in a vacuum."

Already many items were mass-produced by advanced machinery. Some of the new flourishes and profiles appearing on veranda brackets in New Zealand looked very similar to American designs — too similar to have been created independently. Britain offered little of a similar nature (even if the English Picturesque had probably initiated many of the ideas a century before): extensive use of wood for external decoration was not undertaken in Britain, for practical and economic reasons if for none other.

The obvious question must be asked: did San Francisco's flourish and style in the 1870s catch our forebears' imagination — for they *must* have known about it — and thus excite an impulse to emulate it? Her house style must have presented just the symbol of buoyant vitality and success that New Zealanders sought. Already during the previous three decades they had absorbed decorated Gothic Revival houses, many with a distinctive American flair under the auspices of Downing, Davis and others. Now there was an increasing enrichment of their wooden Italianate-type houses as that style gained ascendancy — also with a clear American flavour. Had New Zealand, in fact, found a good neighbour with a style that spelt success? If so, its wider expression would be encouraged during the rest of the 19th century by entrepreneurial American merchants, ever seeking new outlets, in their persuasive marketing of products from their mechanised building-supply industries.

Pl. 9 *(above) Mission house at Mangungu, Hokianga Harbour. Built in 1838, it calmly typifies the basic form of countless ordinary New Zealand houses through 75 years.*

Pl. 10 *(right) Oneida (architect: G.F. Allen), Fordell, near Wanganui, 1869. A brilliant composition, with a spirited Gothic élan in a cascade of gables and steep roof angles.*

Pl. 11 *(above) Not a South Island 1860s mining town, but one at Georgetown, Colorado. A familiar, stiffly upright, Victorian character in pioneer buildings with weatherboarded walls and wooden shop fronts.*

Pl. 12 *(top right) Group of houses in Wright Street, Wellington, 1905. Distinctive rhythm of splayed bays under bracketed gables or hipped peak roofs, elaborate porches with "oriental" arches and balustrades, all with strong resemblances to San Francisco's narrow-frontaged, wooden Victorian houses.*

Pl. 13 *(right) Houses in Steiner Street, San Francisco, 1894. Richly modelled and magnificent, this famous row in American Queen Anne style has broad, splayed bays and shallow porches under full-width bracketed gables. The view, without change, could be of a New Zealand urban area.*

Pl. 14 *(above) Houses in 17th Street, Sacramento, California, c 1885–1890. These simple Stick Style gabled bay cottages are direct counterparts of New Zealand's normal Victorian bay villas. Many are built on raised basements to avoid low-lying humidity.*

Pl. 15 *(left) Bay villa in Masons Avenue, Herne Bay, Auckland, early 1900s. A lavish bay on a large villa. Double-hung windows are continuous across the faces of the bay, with upper grids of coloured glass in the Queen Anne manner. Surface-carved brackets and a scalloped gable end add further flourishes.*

Parallel development or a shared lineage?

NEW Zealand and California, by the 1870s, appear on occasion to have arrived at surprisingly similar forms in a number of their more unsophis-   **80** ticated and relatively unadorned house types. How did it come about that they were so alike? It might be contended that these unexpected like-nesses could have arisen quite independently through parallel develop-ment. Also, that the matching outcomes could have been due to similarity of conditions in the two pioneering societies, as well as to the occurrence of those predictable or "obvious" geometries that arise spontaneously from universal folk forces (as discussed in Chapter 1).

Given the similar components of these modest houses in both countries, with their framed construction, wooden sheathings, lightweight roofing materials at moderate slopes (in response to mild climates), wide, sheltered porches and few rooms, as well as the prevalence of single-storey, detached house types, it might be held that some similarities would be bound to arise, without implying any direct cross-influence between New Zealand and America. Up to a point this does appear to be so: certainly, parallels of types do occur among folk forms, such as the rectangular hut or cabin family, to an upper limit about the size of a relatively bare three- or four-roomed cottage. At this basic level there are similar types of unsophisticated houses across both countries, extending unchanged through several decades before and after 1870.

However, of the slightly more stylised types, the asymmetrical, Gothic-gabled cottage in both countries derives largely from the English Picturesque, while New Zealand's symmetrical, four-square, hipped and verandaed cottage has a lineage from English Georgian planforms and style, as also do certain common American types. (Studies made in

80. *Hillside houses in Los Angeles, c 1880. Several of the small cottages bear strong resemblances to our commonest types in New Zealand. They are found equally in the southern United States.*

81. *Wellington housing patterns, Newtown, c 1905. By the late 19th century, inner suburbs of Wellington and Auckland looked like no English town — but they could be taken for many an American one.*

several of the southern states — North Carolina, Alabama, etc. — identify a similar vernacular house type, with classic, symmetrical plan, central hallway and hipped roof, as a reduced version of the Georgian mansions built in England's early American colonies.) I suggest, then, that the near equivalence of these elementary but stylised house forms in New Zealand and America came about simply because, in both countries, the basic types were taken up from the same English heritage. After all, both New Zealand and America on the whole had continued to look to English styles for stimulus during much of the 19th century. That is not to say that the results resembled English houses, though: the external materials alone saw to that.[11]

Builders, working along pragmatic lines, had gradually developed the norms among common houses in New Zealand. Given constraints of terrain, climate, subdivisions and the materials locally available, their house plans and design style were a combination of inherited "colonial" and of common-sense "folk" practices. At the same time in western America much the same pattern was taking shape, with visibly much the same results — under pioneering conditions similar to our own. The towns in the American West were as newly settled and developing at the same time as those in New Zealand. Panoramas across larger towns in New Zealand show a profusion of wooden houses in a wide diversity of type-forms — with apparent affinities to many in the United States. By the 1890s, New Zealand towns looked no more like English towns than did the new American ones in the West.

However, a fresh factor does emerge when we look at newly developing, even more stylised houses. It is notable that specific designs of features and styled details, particularly in wooden ornamentation, tended

81

82. *Cottages on Los Angeles' outskirts, c 1890. Stylised cottages with a striking similarity to modest, common types in New Zealand, sharing gables, verandas, brackets, lean-to, privy and pickets — plus remarkable formal gardens.*

83. *Victorian cottage and veranda in New Zealand, c 1885. A counterpart, with more than chance likeness, to the stylised American cottages seen in the above illustration.*

82, 83   to become more alike in New Zealand and America the more elaborate the houses became. Eventually, combinations of stylised features and decorative details appeared that were virtually the same in both places. The possibility that this outcome could have occurred by chance, without some direct connection, is remote. Nor can such close similarities have arisen, in isolation, by some process of parallel development.

From about this time, then, New Zealanders must have been familiar with recent American house types and styles and found how relevant, attractive and usable some of them could be. If, in previous decades, everyday New Zealand houses occasionally turned out to be similar to Californian counterparts, the explanation of a development from a joint British heritage could suffice. But from the latter 1870s onwards, I believe the evidence shows that New Zealanders, while continuing on the foundation of previous development, took a clear deviation towards certain American popular house styles of the times.

Italianates on the Pacific

I have already described John Nash's introduction of the Italianate style in England as early as 1802 and its establishment in US house styles by the 1840s. In New Zealand it was adopted officially in colonial architect William Clayton's 1869 design for Government House in Wellington. John Stacpoole, in his *Colonial Architecture in New Zealand* (1976), described this as "a handsome Italianate building. . . The style adapted well to timber construction and became very fashionable in Wellington in the next decade." Its vertical repetitions in window features and stepped, square tower gave it an emphatic but dignified "wooden" character, which influenced other public buildings of the time. In the domestic field, however, few features traceable to it are conspicuous in the standard Italianate houses of our populace: their source was evident elsewhere, most notably in the region of San Francisco.

Simple elements of the style were introduced on New Zealand houses during the 1860s, showing round-arched window heads on double-hung

84   sashes, often in pairs, beneath lowish, 30-degree gables with open eaves lines. A favoured window for main rooms had a large, double-hung sash flanked on the same plane by narrow ones only a third of its width, forming a square in total. It was often projected as a bay, repeating the narrow sashes on its sides. Other forms of rectangular bay windows were also in use, most commonly with a pair of the style's typical flat-arch-headed double-hungs in front. But the splayed bay window, having persisted through the Gothic Revival, retained the appeal of its panoramic view out from within, and was developed to become the Italianate window *par excellence*, in New Zealand as in America.

Today, if you cross San Francisco Bay to visit Oakland, Alameda and Berkeley, you get a clear impression of the kinds of Italianate houses that must have caught our forebears' attention. The 8 km Bay Bridge takes you to these East Bay cities; but 125 years ago you would have shared a ferry from the Embarcadero with businessmen going home to relaxed

84. *Italianate gables in Coromandel Street, Wellington, c 1880. An engaging double house with an off-beat composition of paired Italianate windows and decorated gable peaks.*

suburbs among oak groves, or to the railroad terminal in Oakland at the mainland's edge (the starting point for all New Zealand travellers into the continent by rail). Today in this substantial district of half a million people, several thousands of mid- (and later) Victorian houses have survived. Spared the devastating fire in San Francisco that followed the 1906 earthquake, one- and two-storeyed wooden dwellings, freestanding on their own lots, are arrayed along 50 or a 100 notable streets in endless diversity. Many have suffered neglect or mutilation, and neighbourhoods in many parts are run down; but the total aspect would feel uncannily familiar to any New Zealander, in its details as much as in the panorama. In this single continuous district can be found most of the types and styles of common Victorian houses known to us in New Zealand to the end of the last century and beyond.

In her book *The Ultimate Victorians*, about life in the East Bay, Elinor Richey wrote in 1970: "Victorian domestic architecture reached its ultimate expression in those suburbs that lie on the continental side of San Francisco Bay." Before 1870 most of the district (now Alameda County) had been a pastoral community. Its residential development moved swiftly from weekend cottages and country estates into a genteel suburb. In contrast to San Francisco's cramped sites, which led to her characteristic houses, the land here was spacious and level, allowing expansive house plans and sites gardened for pleasure. (Exotic shrubs and trees from "such places as New Zealand, Africa, South America . . . grew like natives".) In the 1870s a typical rural subdivision offered quarter-hectare lots (over half an acre), each with an orchard at its rear. A typical lot size in an Oakland town subdivision of 1869 was a little over 50 ft. by 120 ft. (15 m by 36.5 m), while 20 years later a normal size was about 40 ft. by 100 ft. (12 m by 30.5 m). These East Bay house sites are of similar scale to typical New Zealand lots surrounding the centre of towns and in later suburbs, with similar effect on the sizes and siting of the resulting houses.[12]

The main elements of the Italianate houses in the East Bay were shared with 'Frisco across the water but were handled more quietly and on a lesser scale. Double-storeyed bay windows were less ostentatious, sur-

85. *West Oakland, California (transcontinental terminus of Union Pacific Rail) in the 1890s. A panorama of two-storeyed houses resembling many areas in New Zealand cities with wooden, rusticated, bracketed, hip-roofed houses and their Italianate bays.*

85

86

95

86. *Single-storeyed development c 1910 in Island Bay, Wellington. Served by the extended tramway system, this new outer suburb is directly comparable with Californian counterparts in the houses and their siting.*

87. *Italianate houses in 8th Street, West Oakland, California, from 1878. These are normal houses of the working suburb seen in an earlier illustration (**85**): two-storeyed bay windows with their bracketed cornices were innumerable.*

87, 88

face decorations and general proportions less strident, and the cresting cornices less overbearing, the roofs being more generally exposed to view. The East Bay community was more relaxed, less flamboyant; and this showed in its houses, which were regarded as distinctly different in style from the row houses of San Francisco. In its social mix and lower density, the East Bay community in the 1870s appears to have been equivalent to the communities of established towns in New Zealand at the time. A reading of the marked similarities between several significant house types that the two places have in common would suggest that this point was not overlooked by New Zealanders. Among such houses are the regular two-storeyed, weatherboarded, bay-windowed and hip-roofed Italianates which represented the majority of standard town dwellings in both localities.

I mentioned earlier that the splayed bay window became a major Italianate feature both in New Zealand and in America. Its range of forms typifies the generally united style that emerges when one considers the Italianate house in the two countries. In fact, a description of the leading characteristics of typical New Zealand houses in the style will take us a long way towards reviewing the general Californian types as well.

88. *Italianate semi-detached house in Coromandel Street, Wellington, 1890s. The same elements as in Oakland (see **85**, **87**, **90**) are here employed on a double house type.*

We can let the conspicuous bay window set the theme. Appearing first with plain facing boards on the weight boxes, which abutted at the splayed corners, and crowned by a simple moulded cornice, this upright, part-octagonal window projection was gradually enriched with a scheme of wooden ornamentation. Most other openings (at least on the "front") also had decorative surrounds, which could be chosen from a variety of profiled boards and cappings for the standard sizes of windows. Shaped blocks were often fixed under the sill ends, occasionally with a convolute-edged apron board below the sill.

79

89, 90

On single-storeyed cottages as on two-storeyed town houses, the building's walls were covered with broad, flat, channeled boards, lapped horizontally, and known in both countries as "rusticated" in imitation of stonework courses. Main corners were emphasised by wide, vertical cover boards, often elaborated as pilasters with moulded panels; or bold, short planks were stepped up the corners to give the weighty appearance of

89. *Typical Italianate bays, Brougham Street, Wellington, 1890s. Pipe-like colonettes at the splays have turned Gothic capitals and bases, cornices are panelled and bracketed, windows segment-topped. Main corners display quoin blocks or panelled pilasters.*

90. *Italianate house, 18th Street, Oakland, California, 1878. Typical of the East Bay, this house carries all the hallmarks of the American wooden Italianates in a modest form. The side bay and peak-hipped roofs appear also in New Zealand. (The sashes are modern.)*

stone quoins. At the top of the walls ran a deep, flat frieze band, under-lined by a moulding; and a vibrant rhythm was set up by tall, curvaceous eaves brackets, fixed at intervals to the frieze, often with moulded panels in between. The underside of the eaves was boarded level, projecting about 12 in. (300 mm). Roofs were normally hipped throughout, with few gables, and at a moderate pitch, displaying a sharply chiselled geometry of planes intersecting at hips and valleys. In New Zealand the roofing material practically everywhere was corrugated iron sheeting, capped by roll-topped ridging and painted universally a deep ox-blood red. In the United States corrugated iron was very seldom acceptable on houses: split redwood shakes (or sawn shingles) were their standard, with occasional use of seamed, flat tin sheeting, slates or similar tiling.

The most characteristic of Italianate-style houses in New Zealand, as well as in the East Bay cities opposite San Francisco, would be the two-storeyed, boxy, wooden houses with bay windows and lowish-pitched, hipped roofs, on relatively narrow frontages. We know them in several cities, Wellington in particular. Tall, upright, dignified — even though markedly asymmetrical with their focal bay window offset to one side and the entrance porch to the other — they stood in ranks along older streets of the inner city and nearest suburbs from the 1880s onwards. They were also the basic stock of many Californian towns after 1870, if pan-oramas photographed in the 1890s are taken as a guide. Their layout of rooms was not unlike the standard English house plans of the period: two rooms in depth to one side of a stair hallway.

However, the freestanding boxy houses with their ornate, all-wooden exteriors as described above were never an English house norm. One **91** might say that the body of the house and its internal layout were much along English lines, but the clothes the New Zealand body wore were

91. *Semidetached house in Southwell, Nottinghamshire, 1900. This typical English counterpart of houses seen in the illustrations opposite is much smaller in scale and height, and totally different in character. It shows continuity with the late-Victorian standard terraced houses.*

American-designed. The American style of elaborately ornamented, bay-windowed, high wooden villas gave expression to Victorian society's pride in property, on both sides of the Pacific, and allowed a degree of ostentation which appealed to the image of the self-made man, a figure typical of the age.

Whatever the variety of causes that may be adduced and debated, the fact is that common New Zealand houses after about 1880 did closely resemble in style the Victorian houses of the region around San Francisco Bay. Certainly, the grand houses of San Francisco itself — those notable centenarian "painted ladies", today revived in all their colourful finery — represented a particular peak, an explosion of ebullience, in houses of an intricacy and florid elaboration that reached beyond much that was seen later in New Zealand. But the initial spark that ignited our forebears' interest without doubt came from there. I have suggested, however, that it was more likely to have been in the East Bay cities that immediate models caught their attention, as more "normal" offshoots from the San Francisco style. We unfortunately cannot know, because of the 1906 fire, just what similarly convincing and moderate house examples might have been familiar to New Zealand visitors in the older streets of San Francisco itself, during some 30 years before their destruction. (Some 2–300 inner city blocks, containing more than 12,000 wooden Victorian houses, were completely razed.)

The East Bay cities still show clearly the general scope of the everyday houses that were typical throughout the Bay area at the time. It would be oversimplifying things to imply that the style of the Bay area was unique in America — far from it; but it had developed auspiciously and with considerable vigour there. Its ready accessibility to New Zealanders, in this location compared with other parts of the States, would also have played a part.

The style was capable of all grades of expression, from pompously ornate to simply well mannered, from grand to modest in scale. Elaboration of the bays, eaves and porch gave individualism free range. The main house forms were strongly sculptural and lent themselves to effective combinations: bay window under gable, two-storeyed stack of splayed bays, splayed bay on top of squared bay, hip-roofed bay or square bay angled across a corner. The recognisable forms underlying these elements did not change much, but their details gradually evolved to live together, enabling a kind of additive designing without undue effort on the builder's part. The applied decoration both intrigued the eye and emphasised the main parts of each house. It was an economical and flexible design system, using virtually standard plan layouts and combining a wide range of interrelated parts.

Built as a rule speculatively and sometimes in tracts, groups of half a dozen houses were often the same in plan and design. In some cases changes would be rung by alternating sets of features on houses along the street, or simply by "mirroring" a standard plan. A considerable degree of uniformity with one's neighbour was accepted in the common man's house — willingly or not — even for quite substantial dwellings. But there was

the opportunity to make a house distinct by individual choices from the wide range of mass-produced woodwork items available from timber merchants' yards.

A wealth of combinations of these Italianate elements was gradually developed in New Zealand to become the basis of our most common Victorian houses through the latter decades of the 19th century. The full-width veranda of the single-storeyed, four-square, hipped cottage was often reduced in length by projecting one main room forward and fronting it with an Italianate window, flush, splayed or squared — an early form of our so-called bay villa. Another type, more common in cooler zones such as Wellington and Dunedin, has the veranda further reduced to a central porch between projecting bay windows on both sides. Again, in each case, there are closely comparable single-storey types among the common Victorian houses in California: the nascent bay-villa form occurs as unsung farmhouses in the original rural areas and valleys around the Bay area (and further afield in other states), while the doubled bay form is particularly common in the cooler north of the state around Eureka — indeed, at a latitude numerically the same as Wellington's southern line. Adjustments to reality in a local climate have thus modified the dominant style forms in these cases, allowing unobstructed light into rooms and providing a still adequate outdoor sitting place. Indeed, some of Dunedin's double-bay, twin-gabled villas make a further modification to this domi-

54
65

92, 94. *Doubled-bay cottage in Kenwyn Terrace, Wellington, c 1905 (below left), and doubled-bay cottage in G Street, Eureka, North Carolina, c 1890 (below right). In cooler climates the veranda may be reduced to a porch, while the two front rooms acquire matching bays, here with Stick–Eastlake ornamentation.*

92

93

94

nant wooden style by their construction in brick, a readily available material with local Scottish-origin associations.

British Italianates

SINCE virtually all the features described above were interchangeable between the American West and New Zealand, it is significant to note the scarcity in Britain of comparable types of Italianate house at the common man's level. There the style was pursued in stuccoed brick or stone and was developed more as the province of the upper middle class, in the code of social differentiation through house embellishment. By the 1850s the Classical tradition was visibly coarsening under the pressure of materialistic display. Heavy-handed piles, with only slight awareness of picturesque Italian models, were deemed to be fitting residences for "men of property": the elegant balance of house and nature seen at St John's Wood did not prevail. Splayed window bays were, of course, plentiful; but normally they were built of brick or stone, with thick masonry piers at the splay angles and heavy proportions in general.

71

In contrast at this point, it is interesting to note that Australia's involvement with the Italianate remained close to British masonry models. There are few direct counterparts to our wooden, two-storeyed, freestanding Italianate type of house in Australia's development. Australia was not endowed with plentiful forests of suitable construction timber: from early days its house-building economy stood firmly on construction in brick (often stuccoed). From about 1840 woodwork on the face of buildings was banned in cities and most towns: the veranda became generally a cast-iron structure including slender columns, brackets, railings and roof frame, typically between the projecting party walls of brick row houses.

In the second half of the 19th century, major imports of softwood timbers such as Oregon fir and California redwood were used in widespread adoption of wood-framed, iron-roofed, weatherboarded houses, generally single storeyed, on the outer fringes of Australian towns and in the country. In a number of respects these modest villas resembled our own houses and passed through much the same succession of international (including some American) styles. Carpentry finishes were generally like ours; but wooden ornament — mostly in eaves valences and grilles, brackets and balustrades — was less plentiful, more European (Swiss chalet) in flavour, and comparatively naive in development.

Elsewhere in Australia brickwork remained king, either as solid or cavity walls, or as a veneer tied to a timber-framed wall (from the 1850s). Cast-iron filigree continued pre-eminent until the 1890s for decorative veranda brackets, friezes and balustrades. Cast iron had been widely used for such purposes since the Regency in Britain (as well as in New Zealand and in Louisiana), but the patterns were seldom copied for wooden brackets: the lacelike scale and intricate piercings characteristic of cast-iron ornaments, as well as their typical surface sculpting and frilled edges, were not practical for working in the coarser and weaker

65

wood. In the same period New Zealand was using a different equivalent in wooden ornamentation, increasingly and inventively unique in this corner of the world.

Wet and dry construction

HERE we may take up one of the key factors in our story: the significance of "wet" and "dry" methods of construction on building sites. British "wet" methods of house building in the 19th century depended largely upon cementing small units together (such as brickwork) to form the main structure, and of mixing various surfacing and finishing materials with water for application to the masonry shell. Such techniques necessarily involved much handwork and lengthy drying times on the building site. There was little opportunity for working economically on larger units away from the site for simpler assembly on the job; nor for mass preparation of a variety of smaller units (other than bricks) to take advantage of machine techniques. On the other hand, New Zealand's house-building industry was dominated by timber from the start. "Dry" processes of frame construction, and the cladding of walls inside and out (as well as ceilings and floors) with boards, allowed an increasing use of machinery off site in the production of ranges of components for quick, dry, on-site

Bargeboards and gables, from Dunedin Iron and Woodware Co.'s illustrated catalogue of c 1886. A range of fretwork "off-the-hook", in styles from Swiss Cottage icicles to Eastlake radial and floral perforations.

assembly. (New Zealand was even more wood-oriented than America, where wet plastering on laths remained normal for internal surfacing of walls and ceilings.)

This dry-construction factor came to characterise the way both American and New Zealand house building and styles developed. Speed of production on site was the commercial driving force: systematic building was the response. Adoption of light-stud, continuous walling instead of heavy, tenon-jointed frames was the key to rapid erection of the house shell. After that, the system was geared to the dry assembly on site of many parts, selected from a multitude of optional components designed to work together under an "umbrella" style. All were orchestrated to suit **fig. p. 103** the major design elements, such as gable ends, bay windows, verandas, porches, doors, staircases and fireplace surrounds. Increasingly, the components were produced by highly versatile, steam-powered, shafting-and-belt-driven machines instead of by hand.

Plan-book houses and American influence on New Zealand designs

PLAN-BOOK guides, or pattern books, are usually regarded overseas as the chief transmitters of ideas that determined the shape of normal houses. Most of their authors, English and American, in the first half of the 19th century were in effect architects. Some simply expanded on current fashions; others took up new issues and gave leads to improve standards through their designs or built works.

I have already discussed several books by advisers or promoters of one school or another who have influenced the tide of opinion and style, with results felt in New Zealand by the middle of the 19th century. The books generally included full designs for a variety of cottages and larger houses, ranging from new types and forms advocated by the author (as with Downing and Davis) to an encyclopaedic anthology across an eclectic range of styles (as with Loudon), accompanied by informative advice, discussion of aesthetics, and a selection of decorative details drawn to a larger scale. Some of the volumes were lavish and costly, addressed to a chosen clientele. Most of the others were of limited printings and of sufficient cost to make them quite uncommon among colonial builders and their clients — thus reducing their direct influence on the ordinary houses of this country.

By 1850 the output of such books in Britain had died down, but not so in the United States. There, architects continued to produce books of their own designs (often already built), probably more for self-promotion than for their purported educational aims. Books of mid-1860s designs, including George Woodward's *Country Homes* and *Woodward's National Architect*, contain wooden Gothic and Italianate houses closely akin to **95** types in New Zealand, as does Isaac Hobbs' *Villas, Cottages and Other Edifices*. Wellington architect of note F. de J. Clere, writing in 1916 of New Zealand's enterprising Victorian carpenter–architects, said:

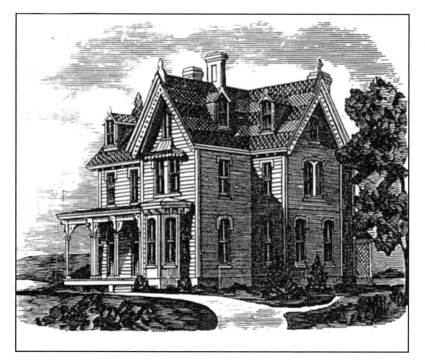

95. *Suburban Residence from Hobbs & Sons' Philadelphia plan book,* Villas, Cottages and Other Edifices, *of 1873. Described as "a plain and ordinary kind of building", it represents a basic American gabled frame-house form, with muted but still-fashionable Gothic attachments.*

"*Woodward's National Architecture* [sic] (an American book . . .) and works of similar kind directed the taste of the day, and the box-shaped house was covered with 'features' nailed all over it. Quoins . . . bay windows and other excrescences were carted from the mills and attached to the fronts; . . . and for some years vulgarity reigned supreme."[13]

In the last quarter of the century, however, the pattern-book initiative shifted to non-architect compilers: builders and plan-book publishers expanded the range with economical and popular editions, some of which were known in New Zealand. Among them, numerous editions produced by the Palliser brothers across 20 years contained extremely competent, wildly eclectic variations on style themes, some of which may have influenced houses here. Their chief legacy was probably as pioneers of a low-cost plan service supplying floor plans and elevations based on the

96. *Plate XII from* Palliser's Model Homes *plan book, published in Connecticut, 1878. The basic gabled frame-house form, similar to Hobbs' design in the illustration above, but more up to date in its surfaces with eastern Stick Style gable features, skeletal porch and batten-panelled walls.*

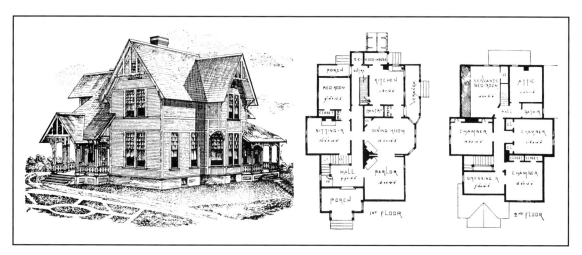

Bay windows, page 227 of R. McMillen & Co.'s catalogue, from Oshkosh, Wisconsin, 1895. A sample of styles in ready-made components, as publicised in volumes issued by supply merchants.

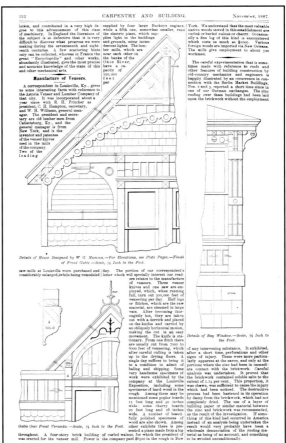

A page from Carpentry and Building *for November 1887, an influential New York monthly which regularly published detailed drawings of current designs by local architects.*

designs illustrated — a practice adopted by New Zealand plan-book compilers in the early 20th century. Others of possible influence include Hussey's *National Cottage Architecture* of 1874, showing simple two-storeyed Italianates of markedly familiar plans and elevations; and Shoppell's large compendium of 1883, *Cooperative Building Plans*, with contributions from many architects, a number of whose designs are directly comparable with standard New Zealand house types, such as the one-and-a-half-storey, L-shaped, gable-bay-and-veranda form. But a volume of this scale would have been rare indeed in New Zealand hands. Few pattern books of note were produced in California until late in the 19th century, whence but little influence came to us by these means.

73

House designs engraved in books, however, were certainly not the only influence in the migration of architectural styles. There were few if any "popular" illustrated house magazines in Victorian days, but knowledge and ideas can travel via personal contacts and by many other means of communication, including the varied vernacular of builders' experiences. Nor is verbatim copying of examples necessary to the diffusion of style ideas: full credit needs to be allowed, at times, for the creative will of the individual to "leap beyond" some example that interested him, modifying its manner to his own purposes. The appeal a style holds in a designer's mind is not usually specific (in that it be simply copied) so much as it offers a special character in shapes, structure and details which he is inspired to equal in solutions of his own. This is a normal process aiding the spread of styles. Builders, on the other hand, tend to borrow ideas more literally from built examples, thus extending the spread of features possibly picked up initially from American journals or from contacts by individuals in their American travels. New and personal versions can then develop without reference to an initial printed source. Influences can thus travel a course of their own and modify local work but no longer be close to the original.

Although certain house designs closely comparable to our own can be found in American plan books, we share many types that cannot. It seems to me that our wide absorbing of American features in our everyday houses occurred in a more pervasive and generalised manner than through individual books, individual houses or, indeed, individual known players. A more convincing process would be that of many factors working together, all of them founded on the normal commercial activity of the house builders (and home acquirers) themselves, controlling aspects of supply and demand in the speculative new-house market, linked to the supporting activity of merchants supplying building materials, and responding to the common people's wishes for up-to-date houses of style and convenience.

In speculative house building, nothing sells that does not either satisfy an existing need or create a desire for itself in the market: at the very least, the chosen American style in shapes and adornments, as offered by the builders, must have satisfied the wishes of home buyers and property owners. The role of the building supply merchants was equally important, in a kind of chicken-and-egg economic dependence and involvement with the builders, who in turn could only build with what-ever materials and products the merchants chose to put on the market. So the builders relied on the merchants to offer a range of fashionable items desirable to the public, while the merchants depended on the builders to guide the home buyers' market choices. In the field of the popular house, it was largely the providers who gave the lead to the public in matters of style. The home buyer's choice was, in fact, limited to the designs made available by both builder and merchant, in judging their appeal to the market. The shifting styles of the period were therefore pursued by the builders and merchants, stimulating a renewal of desirability and demand.

The American plan books of the last Victorian quarter-century did much to standardise house types across the United States, through their comprehensive coverage of current popular house design and wide circu-lation. They would also have played some part in widening the American influence in New Zealand. But the chief means of communication are likely to have been more diverse, including American trade catalogues **fig. p. 106** with patterns of house components obtained from the States by enter-prising builders and supply merchants; their personal contacts through business visits to California, as well as seeing and studying the houses themselves; adoption of American mechanised woodworking and "dry" building techniques, together with the style applications that went with them; and also the stimulus from 1880 of monthly periodicals such as **fig. p. 106** *California Architect and Building News* and *Carpentry and Building* from New York, with their working drawings of detailed features culled from US national house styles. Viewed this way, the whole process of Ameri-**97** can style acquisition becomes more like a gradual and willing osmosis than the result of a few singular events.

97. *House in Marine Parade, Herne Bay, Auckland, c 1900. The sweeping arc of gable ornamentation suggests the possible influence of detailed American drawings, such as on the* Carpentry and Building *magazine page (on page 106).*

Brackets from pattern books and trade catalogues

IN the United States, around the middle of the 19th century, popularisation of the Italianate style, through plan books and by built examples, led to a demand from builders and designers for a stylish range of decorative trimmings for their wooden houses. The growing mid-Victorian taste for greater display and historical effects was the prompt. A particular emphasis was laid on brackets of various kinds, for they were essential to the "bracketed" Italianate style then rising into vogue. Woodworking mills and building supply merchants saw a profitable future in combining steam-power and new American machinery for the mass production of brackets for everyman. Among the machines, the now belt-driven fret (or jig) saws were outstanding. Most versatile from about 1860 was Fay & Co.'s patent Unstrained Scroll Saw, in which a projecting saw blade operated vertically into a guide above the table, allowing free movement of the work — similar in manner to the famous sewing machine popularised in the US by Singer from 1851.

fig. p. 90

The mill companies and merchants could find in contemporary pattern books one source of expertly designed ornaments to put into production: here were ready-made and artistic designs for brackets, balusters, bargeboards, mouldings, cornices, crestings and the like. They were up to date in style and could be adapted for shaping in wood by the newly developed machines. The pattern-book designs could easily be engraved for the merchants' own promotional catalogues. These ephemeral records of 19th-century ornamental design — in the form of old trade catalogues and price lists — have, through their throwaway nature, mostly disappeared. But the scarce survivors, as a rule sequestered in research libraries across America (and New Zealand), are a mine of specific historical information and of fascinating details.

The connections between pattern-book design and the "woodwork-machine shop" may be illustrated best by documents from two of the earliest major participants in the field at the end of the 1850s. Firstly, from Samuel Sloan, a dynamic, articulate and talented Philadelphia architect, who compiled several plan books of larger houses in the 50s and 60s — impressive original designs largely free of the gaucheness of many plan-book makers. He included details of embellishments with each design; and notably in his plan book *Homestead Architecture*, published in 1861, he summarised the character and correct use of various types of wooden brackets for cornices, eaves and verandas, as one of the principal classes of ornament in his day. His experienced comments are supported by drawings of about 20 brackets, appropriately viewed in the solid from below, at an angle.

The second participant — The Brooklyn City Moulding Mill, of Long Island, New York — enters by way of a *Catalog of Patterns* dated 1859, a rare copy of which is held in the Athenaeum of Philadelphia. This volume appears to be one of the first — it is certainly the earliest encountered in

FIG. 133.

FIG. 136.

FIG. 137.

Examples of bracket design by Samuel Sloan, from his Homestead Architecture, *Philadelphia, 1861.*

my research — of that stream of joinery and woodwork trade catalogues through which the impact of machine production was brought to the house-building market. The preface graciously presents the new approach with almost 18th-century formality:

> The subcriber [sic] would respectfully call the attention of Carpenters, Architects, Builders, and all others engaged in business requiring Wood Mouldings, to his large and extensive Stock, and to the different new patterns which he has more recently added to his former Card of Patterns. By the aid of *new and large machinery*, he is prepared to manufacture Mouldings of any pattern or size required, and guarantees in all cases that all Mouldings made at this establishment shall be unsurpassed by any other, *or by hand labour*, and trusts by close attention to his business to merit . . . etc., etc. [my italics].

Ventures such as this, applying new and improved millworking machinery to replace hand work, mark an important turning-point, the outcome of which would deeply affect New Zealand's Victorian houses.

98 The Brooklyn catalogue's wide scope of designs includes ornamental-fretwork vergeboards for Gothic gables and more than 50 brackets in Picturesque Italianate style. About half the bracket designs are freely looping profiles, and the rest are depicted from below at an angle, in just the manner of architect Sloan's bracket drawings: even the line-shading technique is identical to his. The style of many of the brackets is also unmistakably that of Sloan's own examples, whose proper use he described in *Homestead Architecture* published a year or so later. Equally, the decorative vergeboards show more than a hint of the rhythms in Sloan's Gothic Villa designs in his 1852 book, including a specific vertical return at the gable foot.

Might it be that the brackets and other designs for the Brooklyn Mill catalogue had, indeed, been commissioned from Sloan or drawn under his authority? They were certainly of high quality and lasting in appeal. The Brooklyn range of brackets and verges was still being copied by the

98. *Bracket patterns, page 68 of the Brooklyn City Moulding Mill's* Catalog of Patterns *for 1859, Brooklyn, New York. One of four pages of bracket designs, either fretsawn from the solid or built up with two pierced layers on a solid core.*

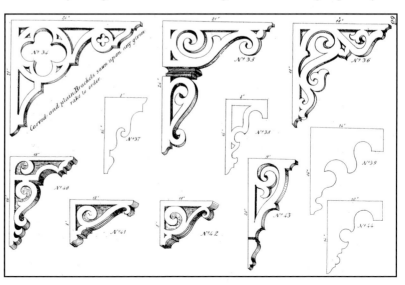

99. *"Designs for Scrolls and Brackets", part of Plate 35 from* Bicknell's Detail, Cottage and Constructive Architecture, *New York, 1873. At least one-third of the patterns collected on the plate are the same as the Brooklyn Mill's catalogue designs of 1859.*

trade verbatim in the 1880s, as demonstrated by the catalogue of the Standard Wood Turning Company, New Jersey, held in the du Pont Winterthur Museum at Wilmington, Delaware. In reverse, *Bicknell's Detail, Cottage and Constructive Architecture*, an 1873 New York architect's pattern book, plainly copied one third of its 50 "Designs for Scrolls and Brackets" from the Brooklyn Mill's designs of 1859. (The conventions of line shading and drawing of brackets from below even persisted past the 19th century: eaves brackets were still shown in this way in Auckland's Kauri Timber Company catalogue in 1913.)

99

The fascination with brackets and scrollwork, prevailing throughout the whole Victorian era, provides many clues to the popular expression of the spirit of the times, changing across the century. It may be used as a guiding line, like Ariadne's thread, through the labyrinth of shifting Victorian fashions — ever present and articulate. Brackets, of one kind or another, were an essential part of the Victorian house's external character. Repeated under eaves, below cornices on bay windows, at the head of posts to porches and verandas, at the top of main corners or under the foot of projecting gables, under the gable panels themselves — brackets were legion. Strip a Victorian house of its multitude of brackets and the magic has gone. The major forms of the house, its geometrical cubes and recesses, remain but are mute. Its brackets give it scale and variety of detail, a personality and life of its own.

fig. p. 112
100

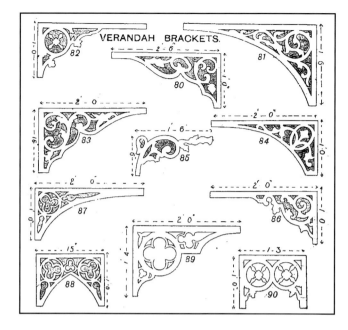

Veranda brackets, from the Kauri Timber Co. Ltd's catalogue for 1913, Auckland. Designs evidently remained available for several decades, with others added as styles changed.

From stone into wood

100. *House in Mt Eden, Auckland, c 1895. Every item of ornament on this fully bracketed bay villa can be traced to catalogue pages of the Kauri Timber Co. Ltd — including bargeboards and the entire bay window.*

THE early millwork catalogues described above arose largely from East Coast translations into wood of the current European styles, expanded by the infinite variations of shape possible in scrollwork. The Brooklyn Mill's catalogue of 1859 serves to show the process in action, converting the stone form of Classical console brackets into carved wooden versions. These engraved drawings have a sketchiness of fresh creation about them in comparison with the precision of later definitive steel engravings, unchanged thereafter. Scrolled patterns were adopted from the surfaces of consoles, from Jacobean flat "strapwork" ornamentation and from Georgian stair-tread ends for use as thin fret-sawn and pierced brackets in the adornment of the Victorian veranda. Gothic forms were

likewise converted for brackets, usually from window tracery or decorated spandrel wall panels, with some guidance (though not extensive) from the Pugin family's measured drawings of 1810 to the 1830s.

Judged by the quality of the initial designs for brackets and other components shown in early catalogues, it appears likely that these machine products were not simply commercial efforts by amateurs but were designed by talented American architects of the time. The accusation often made in our own time, of a lowering of "taste" in popular housing by manufacturers and builders seeking to make products which appealed to the "uncultured masses" and their "innate love of richness and decoration", would need reviewing if this indeed be the case. This is of considerable interest to New Zealand, where the continuation of these types of components in trade catalogues set the standard for design quality of the everyday builders' houses. Although the application of these ornamental enrichments to individualise our houses lay in the field of "popular art", many of the basic patterns themselves are far from being naive or clumsy versions of historical designs, suggesting the presence of expert and lettered sources in their making. Possibly New Zealand architects were involved in the design of the further ranges of decorative components for local merchants, as seen in their trade catalogues.

101

101. *Archway spandrel panel, South Porch, Gloucester Cathedral, late 15th century. One source of the standard "quatrefoil and dagger" pattern adopted for scrollsaw-cut veranda brackets in many variations.*

Machine-made America

THE contrast between American technical advances and European practice is underlined by a report in the *California Architect and Building Review* of August 1880:

> Machine-made doors of American manufacture . . . are recognised as superior to the more expensive hand-work of the foreign mechanics [tradesmen], and their general adoption by builders in foreign parts is, no doubt, a severe blow to the carpenters of those lands. It will take some time, however, before the severely-conservative people of Europe will as universally accept machine-made work as Americans do. A love of old customs and old things, in the old world, will have a retarding influence against the wholesale use of machine-made work.

In New Zealand, enterprising businessmen in the 1870s do not appear to have been retarded by such feelings. Our larger builders and building supply merchants had become interested in American production techniques and were soon importing advanced woodworking machines from there as well as from British suppliers, who had by now taken up the earlier American lead in developing their ordinary joinery machines. Possibly the American machines, such as their scroll saws and moulders, were accompanied by templates similar to the popular Victorian device of stencil guides, cut with designs they were capable of producing — although I have found no trace of such ephemera. One could expect that the Americans' gift for the marketing of images with popular

102

fig. p. 114

102. *"Six-Inch Four-Sided Molder" built by Rogers & Co. in Connecticut: a state-of-the-art machine of 1893 for quick and versatile shaping of joinery members.*

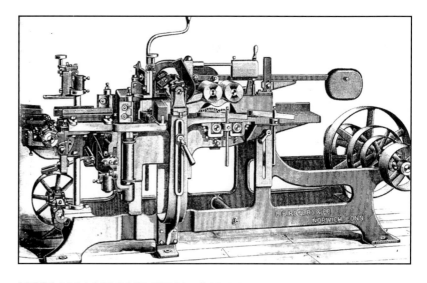

Gothic-Italianate bay window unit, Type 4, from the Kauri Timber Co. Ltd's catalogue for 1913, Auckland. A mid-Victorian shop-assembly in large units, aided by machine production.

appeal, and their genius in communication and "follow-up" services, would ensure that customers were kept up to date with the latest trends.

The 1874 *Illustrated Catalogue* of the Dunedin firm Findlay & Co. offered "Sashes made to order and forwarded to any part of the Colony", and showed four standard designs for double-hung sashes. Interestingly, the catalogue heading of "Sash, Door and Blind Factory" gives a clue to American emulation, this being in fact the stock US wording for such factories, in use in trade associations and catalogues.

It is known that American doors were being imported into New Zealand by the 1860s: Lady Barker's letters of 1866 in *Station Life in New Zealand* mention "doors readymade from America" being supplied from a timber yard in Christchurch for their precut house 50 miles (80 km) out of town. Moreover, the general extent of New Zealand's contact and exchange with West Coast America may be gauged by another extract from the report quoted above, in the *California Architect and Building Review* of August 1880. Reviewing the United States' export trade in panel doors and sashes, the report states: "Last year [1879]

California alone shipped as many as 28,000 doors in one month to New Zealand and Australia."

This would be a very large delivery of doors even if it was for the whole year!

New Zealand follows suit

NEW Zealand businessmen of larger companies in the 1880s, such as the Kauri Timber Company in Auckland and Findlay's Dunedin Iron and Woodware Company, took notice of American-styled details and introduced versions of them into their catalogues. From this time onward, trade catalogues of New Zealand joinery and timber merchants bear strong resemblance to their American counterparts in their manner of drawing and displaying items. But it was not only their presentation that was similar: the objects shown were in many cases of identical design to American examples. As a case in point, a page from a turn-of-the-century catalogue of Prouse Bros. & Co., timber merchants of Wellington, makes an informative study. A compendium of popular brackets from previous

103

103. *Bracket patterns, page 28 of Prouse Bros. & Co.'s* Catalogue of Mouldings *for 1904, Wellington. In the central column, the three top brackets and one at foot are among those identical to American designs of 1859 and 1876.*

115

decades for veranda posts or under gables, this typical selection of Victorian designs is mostly based on convolutions of leafy, scrolled tendrils, classical in manner. A few geometric patterns as well are derived from Gothic tracery, as found in corner panels above the arches of doorways and nave arcades — for example, at Canterbury Cathedral in Kent.

It is significant that very close matches can be found between the Wellington catalogue brackets and American bracket designs. The American sources generally predate the New Zealand catalogue by 30 or so years. Among the 19 brackets shown on the Wellington 1904 Prouse catalogue page, five have been traced to identical brackets in American trade catalogues. Of these five identical matches, two appear in the Brooklyn City Moulding Mill's catalogue of 1859, two can be found in the 1876 catalogue of D.A. Macdonald & Co.'s mill in San Francisco, and one is in the S.A. Brown Sash & Door Co.'s catalogue of 1886 from Chicago. A further five scrolls closely resemble American types in catalogues from the 1870s; two others I have seen in the States; and two "lobed" designs are in a common US style.

This strike rate of 15 out of 19 examples at random appears sufficient to confirm direct American influence in New Zealand's Victorian house styles. The range of varieties of scrolled shapes that might be used in fretwork brackets is infinite: the S-shaped "spiral" scroll is itself possibly the most universal of man's decorative forms — certainly one of the oldest — and is used in almost every culture from long before the Classical world to our own Polynesia. And the power-driven American scroll saw was now extremely versatile, allowing any curvaceous and pierced

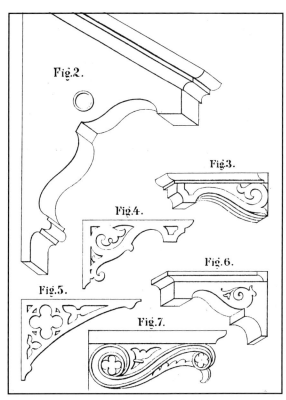

"Brackets and Modillions", part of page 60 from D.A. Macdonald & Co.'s catalogue for 1876. Figures 4 and 5, the only openwork veranda brackets in the book, appear in the Wellington catalogue of Prouse Bros. for 1904 (see **103***) and in an earlier (undated) edition.*

pattern to be invented and cut at will. Given this prolific range of patterns and the infinite possibilities available in shape and detail, close matches of this order cannot be matters of coincidence. More matches would no doubt have been possible during Victorian times between many other catalogues or built examples, bearing in mind the rate of losses to both during the past 100 years and more.

The D.A. Macdonald & Co. catalogue mentioned above is a notable example of trade literature from the American West Coast — one of the most beautiful of catalogues, elegantly presented in shadow-line engraving. The Bancroft Library in Berkeley holds a copy of the firm's Enterprise Mill issue of 1876, which provides a most telling comparison with the Wellington catalogue page. Factors that link the Wellington Prouse brackets to those of the San Francisco Macdonald catalogue seem conclusive in several ways: the two New Zealand brackets, both commonly used in this country (one from Gothic tracery, one an Italianate scroll), are essentially identical to the two Macdonald brackets in their shape, proportion and curvature; they adjoin each other on the pages of both catalogues and their relative size is the same in both pairs; the style of shadow-line engraving is identical in both catalogues; and, moreover, the images of both designs are reversed in the Wellington catalogue but the direction of light for the shadow lines remains from upper left, as is the normal convention — exactly as would occur if a copy were engraved directly. As said so often in this book, a Californian source is the most likely. The alternative explanation, that both brackets were drawn in New Zealand, simultaneously, from some other (non-American) source, is hardly credible.

It might also be asked where Macdonald & Co. obtained the designs for their catalogue. Could they find, in the relatively uncouth San Francisco of the 1870s, talents capable of creating designs of such sensibility, let alone the skills to cut engravings of such beauty? Or did they look to the East for this degree of sophistication? No doubt there were architects other than Samuel Sloan with a flair for bracket design whom they might have engaged. Or, dare we ask, may Sloan's hand be seen behind *these* characterful designs? The "feeling" and fleshy rhythms of the foliage profiles are exactly his, as is the manner of drawing — all evidenced by the details of Designs I and V of his *City and Suburban Architect* of 1859.

It is perhaps significant, also, that neither Bicknell's pattern book of 1873, *Detail, Cottage and Constructive Architecture* (which contains several pages crowded with bracket designs), nor any other major American pattern book has proved to be the direct source for other common New Zealand brackets. This further suggests that such pattern books were not widely known here, and that the (now rare) trade catalogues — if not, indeed, actual imported brackets themselves — were the likely source of many of our bracket designs. By 1880, as I have mentioned, importers were bringing in American-made doors, windows, hardware, ornamental features, brackets, etc. complete. All of these could readily be applied to houses already similar in design to many American types.

Brackets Nos. 415 and 417 extracted from Prouse Bros. catalogue page (see **103***) and reversed to match figures 4 and 5 of the Macdonald catalogue (see figure opposite).*

104

99

104. *"Urns and Brackets",* page 63 *of D.A. Macdonald & Co.'s* Catalog of Doors, Sashes and Blinds *for 1876, San Francisco. Extraordinary elegance for a commercial promotion of wooden brackets and knobs.*

American clothes

INSIDE the house, normal English-type components and finishings continued to be used with little change. Apart from imports such as doors and other special items, the nature of interior joinery work and wooden trim, such as skirtings and cornices, architraves and panel moulds, balustrades and so on, remained close to standard British profiles and patterns, albeit without great variety and somewhat simplified. Certainly, few matches with American profiles can be found among the vast range of full-size section drawings shown in catalogues such as the turn-of-the-century Chicago-based *Official Moulding Book (Illustrated)*. Given the wooden exteriors of New Zealand houses, however, there was little by way of a current model in British practice for their exterior design and wooden finishings, particularly in their ornamentation. In this field the American sources offered ready-made, practical and attractive solutions. Hence our houses remained traditional enough, in a British sense, internally as far as their basic room layout and finishings were concerned; but they were clothed externally in what amounted to American Victorian styles. Thus we achieved a fresh amalgam in our locally available materials: a compound of both British and American influences.

It should not be supposed, however, that our forebears were attracted

105. *Wooden Classical house, Whangaimoana, near Martinborough, Wellington, 1876. Every detail of traditional stone-work was meticulously reproduced in wood. To the owner of this patrician house, the style's appeal was worth the effort entailed.*

to American houses solely because they were built in timber. Wooden-framed and wooden-boarded houses had long been built in Scandinavia, the Balkans, Turkey and elsewhere, all with their own appealing characters; but none was taken up as a direct model for houses here. Equally, buildings constructed in stone or brick have many times inspired quite adequate replicas in wood — if their style appealed sufficiently. New Zealand has examples of its own making, from the richly classical **105** Whangaimoana house — a Renaissance palazzo in miniature — to our **168** innumerable weatherboarded houses modelled on brick-walled English Arts and Crafts houses from the turn of the century.

It was not, therefore, simply because they were built in brick or stone that Britain's 19th-century housing styles were often bypassed in New Zealand. Reasons no doubt included rejection of the oppressive types of row houses experienced in British towns and villages and their undesirability in our more open town layouts and subdivision patterns. Again, their dour style was hardly an appealing image for life in a new country. **69** The principal differences between various British and New Zealand house types are not only differences of materials and methods but also the differences in human aims and ideals of a pioneering outlook, which led in turn to differences of style. The style of the new American houses, of one or two storeys freestanding on their plots, was seen to be attractive in meeting many of those aims.

In the last 20 years of the 19th century, circumstances had brought these two young and vigorous Pacific neighbours into closer contact, widening the range of our exposure to adventuresome American building styles as they developed. At many levels we clearly found their new ways to be relevant to our own needs and desires, under directly comparable conditions and in tune with a modern "democratic" spirit. Nowhere was this more evident than in their fresh and inventive wooden house types built for the common man in the latter decades of the 19th century.

Chapter 8

The Anatomy of the Villa

Ornament rules

IT may seem that features and ornaments were chosen and "applied" to New Zealand's common houses in the latter part of the 19th century with more whim than reason. But choices of this kind are made with at least some thought within a context: they do not "just happen". Behind every combination of forms lies a decision made by someone acting in the role of designer, setting out to meet some need or wish. The selection may have been made, of course, with some preconceived images in mind: the vocabulary of a particular "style" generally includes a variety of useful combinations of forms that have been made to work satisfactorily together. **106**

106. *House gable and porch, Somme Parade, Wanganui. An adventurous play of construction and ornamented forms of pierced decoration, and of space in an extraordinary broad-bayed Edwardian design.*

An ultimate case in point would be the Classical Orders, of perfected relationships. In more general usage the selection may have been for a decorative enrichment of the shapes of a villa's gable-and-bay-window combination, or as a welcoming elaboration along the front of a veranda.

It will be obvious that ornament was a central issue in the design of Victorian houses everywhere. Behind its prolific use lay a few rules which are of interest to recall. Firstly from Welby Pugin, the purest Gothic Revivalist, who began his book *True Principles of Pointed or Christian Architecture* (1841) with "two great rules for design":

> 1st, that there should be no features about a building which are not necessary for convenience, construction, or propriety;
>
> 2nd, that all ornament should consist of enrichment of the essential construction of the building.

He berated his times for using ornaments that were "actually constructed", instead of forming the decoration *of construction*, to which "they should be always subservient". (In spite of his apparent strictness, his rules admitted without compromise some of the century's most sumptuous ornamentation in his interiors for the new Houses of Parliament.)

Behind many a traditional decorative form lies a constructional purpose in disguise, a necessary but discordant member decently clothed. It may be a jutting beam carrying a ledge, shaped into a curving leafy volute, or a raking brace transformed into a pierced tracery bracket. But disguise is not a necessary factor: the structural form itself may be enriched without undergoing transformation. In open-eaved gables, for **fig. p. 103** example, an exposed cross tie and king post, repeating the construction within the roof, was often enhanced by added members or decorations; and great medieval timber-roof trusses and arches were effectively enriched by inset carved panels.

From strut to ornate veranda bracket tells the story simply. Basic, light, post-and-beam veranda frames, having little stiffness sideways, could be braced by diagonal struts at the top of the posts — this was raw construction exposed. More elegant solutions lay in cutting the strut to a curve, as was done in Regency style. Further decorative geometry was added by **98** circles in the corner, in turn leading to ornate Gothic tracery forms in the Picturesque manner. With the Italianate came a flowing graciousness in **99** the elaboration of scrolls, foliage and curlicues, filling out the structural triangular form and intriguing the eye.

Pugin's precepts, verging on "functionalism", were far in advance of his time's philosophies. Active practitioners found them hard to reconcile with current styles, such as the Italianate. A succinct American attempt at a middle course was made by Samuel Sloan in his book *The Model Architect*, 10 years after Pugin's, by dividing ornament into two classes:

> 1. Features which belong essentially to the building and are made ornamental by giving them shape and finish;
>
> 2. Those which are not essential to the building but which suggest at once to the mind a need which they appear to supply.

Pl. 16 *Two-storeyed backs of houses, Kenwyn Terrace, Newtown, Wellington, c 1905. Typically one-storeyed at the street, these Wellington hill houses, with dramatic airborne gables, apply Stick Style and Eastlake details with imagination.*

Pl. 17 *House in West 3rd Street, Benicia, San Francisco Bay, c 1885. Exhibiting many familiar features associated with typical New Zealand houses, this personable Stick–Eastlake design has an individual touch of its own.*

The Bay Villa's Countenance

Pl. 18 *1840s – c 1900. Simple sloping bargeboards are fixed on the flush face of the gabled main wall (or fretwork barges stand forward about 12 in. (300 mm)), with a compact bay window — vertically proportioned, splay-sided or squared, with hipped or flat roof — attached centrally on the wall face below, enlarging the room. A mix of Gothic and Italianate features was general. (Constable Street, Newtown, Wellington. See also* **109**.*)*

Pl. 19 *c 1890 –1910. A main triangular "pediment" gable is moved forward to the* face *of a splayed windowed bay, which now occupies the full width of the end of the projecting room, further enlarging it. Broader bargeboards, panelled or scallop-shaped, may stand forward of the gable face by about 12 in. (300 mm). The gable stands above a frieze band, which returns from both corners and continues under the house eaves as normal. The gable's outer corners are "supported" both ways by fretwork cantilever brackets under the frieze, flanking the splayed window sides. Square-ended bay windows were treated similarly. (Ardmore Street, Ponsonby, Auckland.)*

Pl. 20 c *1895–1915. The whole of the gable pediment is projected* beyond *the window bay face and carried on eaves brackets fixed to the frieze face. A strong cornice or eaves gutter along the gable base may connect the feet of the bargeboards, or the bargeboards may project yet further. The widely oversailing upper corners are supported by paired cantilever brackets under the frieze band as before. (Mt St John Avenue, Epsom, Auckland. See also* **Pl. 15** *and* **128.***)*

Detail of Verge Finish in Front Gable.
Scale, ½ Inch to the Foot.

"Verge Finish in Front Gable", detail drawing of house design from March 1888 issue of Carpentry and Building *(New York). Scalloped bargeboards, medallions and turned pendant with crosstie all point to an American style source for New Zealand's prolific gable themes. (Compare with* **Pl. 15***.)*

Pl. 21 c *1900–1915. Finally, the rules are broken and the frieze band is omitted under the gable corners, which are carried on deeper, enlarged brackets (sometimes one way only), taken right up to the eaves line itself. The window heads may be raised (often with a decorated shallow leadlight) and the bargeboards merged ornamentally into a single sweeping form. The proportions stand taller: the dramatic climax is reached. (Masons Avenue, Herne Bay, Auckland.)*

Pl. 22 *(left) Corner bay villa, Upton Street, Herne Bay, c 1910. This assured late Edwardian has near-symmetry on its corner site. Simple Stick Style details of gables and "Chinese" balustrade are softened only by turned veranda posts and slightly profiled brackets.*

Pl. 23 *(below) Bay villas in Masons Avenue, Herne Bay, Auckland, 1900ș. Spacious individuality with a sense of community. A row of smiling villas along a suburban street.*

He gave as examples of the first: chimneys, the ends of rafters, and major brackets; and he included in the second: "the great many brackets which apparently yield support to parts which really do not require it of them" — in other words, which give visual support to eaves, etc. — thus subtly circumventing Pugin's rule and licensing the non-constructional use of the brackets so beloved of the Italianate style.

House and land

THERE is always a sensitive connection between the prevailing lot sizes and the typical house plans in a town, governed mainly by frontage widths. Land value, occupation density, supply and demand, location and social group, all play further parts in determining the resulting house types — in endless variety around the world. Not surprisingly, New Zealand's subdivision practices for house sites are quite comparable with those pursued in California under similar conditions. Both Wellington and San Francisco have hilly sites and a certain extent of flat land near the city centre, and thus tend to be characterised by narrow frontages and fairly dense occupation. This occurred progressively after 1840 in Wellington's case with the eventual subdividing of the 1100 preplanned "town acre" units, but in the case of San Francisco, from the time of its first speculator-driven beginnings.

107. *Inner-city residential panorama, Marjoribanks Street, Wellington, c 1905. The wide variety of wooden house types reflects the vagaries of subdivision of the inner-city "town acre" properties. (See also* **81** *and* **85**.)

San Francisco's combination of factors produced its narrow, vertically compressed, ornate town houses. Wellington's land pressures were less keen, with an extensive area available on Te Aro Flat from the start. **81, 85** Yet even there, Wellington by 1890 was a city with many "up-and-down", narrow, two-storeyed houses crowded together in groups, while open fields remained in areas in between. The small frontages reflected not so much land shortage as those commercial factors under which speculative **107** builders catered for housing needs at differing economic levels: the component of land cost in each house price could be lowered by closer subdivision of the "town acre". Thus our various typical house types were determined largely by frontage widths and land values graded according to the cost levels acceptable to buyers, across the whole social structure.

Two of the commoner proportions for Wellington town acres under the Wakefield scheme, as laid out by surveyor Captain Mein Smith's 1840 plan for the city, were 132 ft. by 330 ft. deep and 160 ft. by 272 ft. deep: (that is, 40 m by 100.5 m and 49 m by 83 m). These units, in multiples, governed the spacing of the original streets. The acre dimensions were readily subdivided into quarter-acre or eighth-acre lots, in two sets, with dimensions respectively of 66 ft. by 165 ft. deep and 40 ft. by 136 ft. deep, the city blocks being usually two lots in depth. Very few lots of such generous scale remain: reality moved far from the ideal, with haphazard and often minuscule subdivision. Common frontages ranged from 50 ft. (15.2 m), through 33 ft. (10 m), 25 ft. (7.6 m), 22 ft. (6.7 m), 20 ft. (6.1 m) and 16 ft. (4.9 m), the last being used for semidetached units. Subdivisions were uncontrolled, resulting in overcrowded slums in parts of our main cities by 1900.[1]

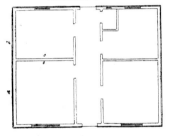

No. 5.—Ground Plan of Four Roomed Cottage.
CHIMNEYS TO BE AT a b or c.

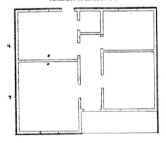

No. 6.—Ground Plan of Four Roomed Cottage.
CHIMNEYS TO BE AT a b or c.

Square and L-front cottage plans from Findlay & Co.'s illustrated catalogue, Dunedin, 1874.

Single-storeyed house plans: cottages and villas

FROM the beginning of the 1880s, new residential areas were opened up on city outskirts, now made accessible by steam- then horse-drawn trams. Privately owned land-holdings were subdivided in localities such as Newtown in Wellington, and Ponsonby and Newton in Auckland. In these fresh fields, somewhat wider subdivision than was usual in the compressed city became common for domestic lots, the greater width allowing the convenience of houses planned on one floor. Certain of the small house types which had been present in cities and towns since the early colonial days continued in these new inner "suburbs". Among **108** them the four-square, symmetrical, hip-roofed cottage, often with bay windows or a veranda across its front, was a basic type; another was the **109** asymmetrical, L-shaped form with a projecting room, often gabled, and with a veranda into the angle. Both have been introduced in previous chapters of this book, the former with links back to English Georgian rural houses and colonial practices, the latter from folk forms stylised after the Picturesque and Gothic Revival movements of Britain and the United States.

108. *Symmetrical "four square" cottage, Sussex Street, Ponsonby, Auckland, 1890s. A standard colonial type with Georgian parentage, this example has later Italianate broad windows. (Entry, chimney and balusters are not original.)*

Together these two cottage types represent by far the commonest of our small, populist Victorian houses, both in towns and in the country. These are the simple, basic houses from which all larger single-storeyed houses developed over time, thus serving most of the social groups and economic gradations of a generally middle-class community. "Four-square with four square rooms", they share the universal New Zealand floor plan — two rooms deep on both sides of a passage straight through the middle, giving independent access to each room, with scullery, bathroom and minor services at the back, usually under a lean-to roof. In the asymmetrical type, projection of the front room could admit a further small bedroom on that side or alternatively under the lean-to, bringing the accommodation to five main rooms plus lesser services across the back.

109. *Asymmetrical cottage with returned veranda, Somme Parade, Wanganui, early 1880s. Pristine and handsomely proportioned, this house in the perennial gable and veranda*
110 *form is finely detailed using Gothic Revival ornament from catalogues.*

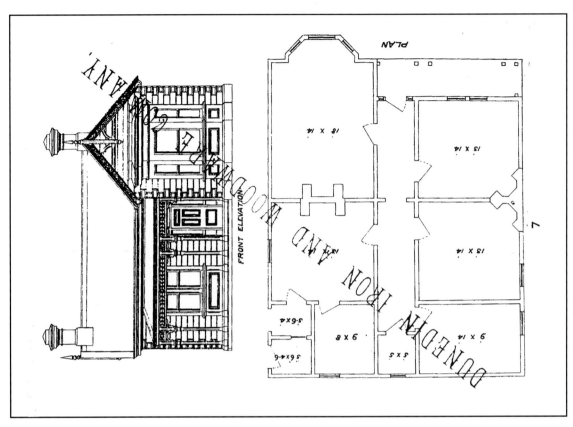

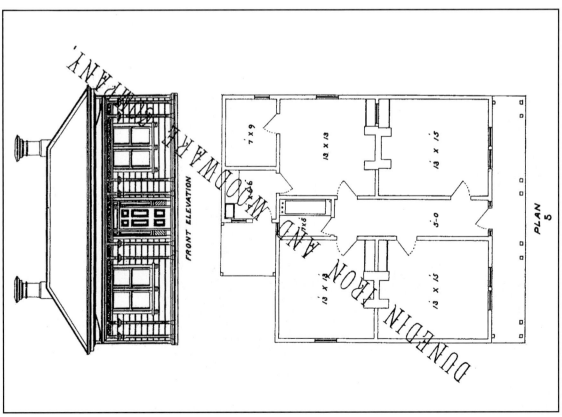

The standard width adopted for rooms on both sides of the entrance hall was 12 ft. (3.65 m). (Occasionally this became 13 ft. (4 m) or, more rarely, 14 ft. (4.3 m).) The hall, in the "social" front portion of the house, was usually 5–6 ft. wide (1.5–1.8 m). It then reduced a little in width, behind a framed archway half-draped with a heavy velvet curtain, marking the "private" zone beyond. The front hall gave access to the "best room", the parlour, which always had to present a tidy state for visitors. The main bedroom matched it on the other side, serving on occasion as a repository for visiting ladies' coats and final adjustments. The kitchen (through the archway, of course) was generous in size, second only to the parlour, and was the family's centre for meals and general activity (until the advent of the dining room in the last decade of the century). A broad, cast-iron cooking range in a brick-and-tiled recess was the room's focus and source of warmth; the kitchen table served a multitude of family needs; and more menial tasks were relegated to the adjoining scullery, wash house or coal store.

Open fireplaces provided heating in some of the other rooms, always including the parlour and the dining room (if there was one). In the North the main bedroom sometimes had a fireplace; in the colder South there was one in most bedrooms. The brick chimneys were normally "internal" in the plan, with the fireplaces back-to-back in the cross partitions to retain maximum heat within the building. Given the lack of insulation in the walls and iron roof, in typical New Zealand manner the closed cellular plan enabled one or two rooms to be heated economically while the rest of the house froze.

The front parlour in the evenings provided the warm hearth for much of home life, particularly in larger families when every room was in demand. Reading, card games, talking and sewing were interspersed with suitable parlour games and music-making, with piano or song. Music

110. *(opposite) Dunedin Iron and Woodware Co.'s catalogues offered stock cottages in the 1880s, with typical floor plans and elevations of the basic New Zealand four- and five-roomed mid-Victorian house. Bedroom fireplaces indicate the cold southern climate.*

111

112

111. *Dining room c 1905 in a villa, as usual with its bay overlooking the side garden. A typical fireplace with crowded mantel shelves, a piano and handy table all indicate the room's general use for family activities.*

112. *Parlour, 1890s.*
A typically high-ceilinged
space, well lit by its bay
window and furnished
for many uses. The piano
shields a comfortable
sitting area which appears
less formal than many
of the time.

was all-important in many Victorian homes: everyone was expected to contribute in some way. On the other hand, "keeping up appearances" must have taxed the busy wife and mother's effort to have the parlour pristine at all times — undoubtedly a deterrent against its full family use.[2]

A code of social customs surrounding the use of the front and back doors reflects the manner of living for which these houses were intended, regardless of size. Centred in this were the rituals of Victorian middle-class social entertaining to which many aspired, involving "calling" and receiving "at home" for afternoon tea, and of sociable evenings with guests. An unexpected caller, or guests invited to visit by note or return of cards, duly presented themselves at the front door and were ushered (by the housemaid, if any) into the parlour to be greeted by their hostess or host.

113 Everything visible was calculated both to welcome and impress the visitor: the whole presentation and ornamentation of the house front, the rich mouldings on the front door itself and its glowing coloured glass, the hall table and hat stand, the elegant main bedroom (for cloaks) and the well-furnished formal parlour.

Use of the back door had its own strong connotations as well. "Familiarity" was the keynote here: you went to the back if using the front door might be seen as "standing on ceremony"; if you were a family member returning or calling in, or were a child (on any purpose); if you were delivering groceries or coal, taking orders or collecting for charity; or if you were a neighbour or close friend dropping in. By this door was

113. *Front entrance to symmetrical cottage, Ardmore Street, Ponsonby, Auckland, 1890s.*
A delicately ornamented veranda offers a gracious welcome to visitors.

the route to the wash house and the sole house toilet attached to it (or else further down the garden). The back door was in constant use, approached by all and sundry. In contrast with the front, however, it received negligible architectural acknowledgement of its major role. Paradoxically, the back-door area was more "public" than the front, yet remarkably little was done to make this area an enjoyable setting. In most cases a rudimentary porch beside the tank stand, and a cramped entry through the scullery, served the family as the unprepossessing usual way into their home.

86

The basic plan described above resulted in a house a minimum of 30 ft. in width (9.15 m). A common lot frontage in the new outlying subdivision areas was 36 ft. (11 m), which suited the standard plan and allowed access down one side to the rear garden and back door. The

114. *Veranda, Mair Street, Whangarei, c 1900. Stylish, riotous — but, on analysis, highly organised. Its features were all in vogue in 1880s US designs — lathe-turned posts, panels of spindles and scroll fretwork, turned drops and face brackets, "Chinese" balustrade grilles and Islamic arches.*

114

115

relatively small scale of the houses and the regular subdivision units, however, led to a monotony of aspect of the whole. Many groups of houses were built only 4 or 5 ft. (1 or 1.5 m) back from the street line, adding to the already dense feeling. At the least they avoided the excessive crowding of numerous inner-city areas, the potential slums of the future.

Styles from overseas

THE adoption of particular styles for New Zealand houses can be seen as deliberate choices, within the eclectic tastes of the Victorian age, to meet people's interests and wishes at the time. Overseas styles did not simply reach New Zealand of their own accord, as a matter of course: they were adopted by someone for good reasons. The questions of why and how such choices were made demands consideration.

The choice from the start rested on overseas models. In house design and in other matters, as the decades passed, New Zealand's enterprising Victorians would have had a mind to emulate models which in some way corresponded with the directions in which they hoped to progress. It seems likely that their choices were made for definable reasons — an appealing style of home or promising building method, whether British or American. What those reasons may have been we will consider as we proceed.

The American single-storeyed house and the climate

TURNING to single-storeyed house types in America we find parallel cases of considerable interest, initially in the older parts of the Eastern states. In the Southeastern states the heritage of their British colonial

130

115. *Veranda, Madison Place, Lexington, Kentucky, c 1890. The style features of the illustration opposite are clearly present, elaborated in squarish panels above the post brackets, scrolled fretwork panel under the eaves, turned posts and heavy, carved face brackets: the architecture of ornament.*

origins shows up in the forms of certain Victorian-styled "folk" houses before 1850. Some of these turn out to be practically indistinguishable from the contemporaneous New Zealand four-square, front-verandaed, hip-roofed cottages which derived from the earlier Georgian and Regency disciplines, as we have seen.

During the 18th century, while they were British colonies, Virginia and the Carolinas had built under the same ruling Georgian style. A principal house form (which later spread far and wide, including through the Midwest) was the two-storeyed, one-room-deep, broad and symmetrical-fronted house with a central hallway between the rooms: a typical formal Georgian layout, often in wood construction, and referred to now as an I-house plan. (Our 1821 Butler/Kemp House, at the Kerikeri mission station in Northland, would belong in this international family.) At a humbler level, the influence of Georgian models even on folk-built houses is seen in the formal symmetry they often sought — because, it was felt, that was what a "proper" building should look like. One version of the I-house plan in the South — reduced to one storey but two rooms in depth — retained the central hall and doorway. This resulting popular cottage type became common in North Carolina particularly, throughout the Victorian period and often with Italianate associations.

Its external appearance is the same as one of our commonest of Victorian cottages, as mentioned above: timber-framed with horizontally boarded walls, symmetrical, low-pitched, peak-hipped roof, wooden veranda across the front, central front door with framed sidelights, double-hung windows and boxed eaves (some with an Italianate frieze band and brackets). The plan is the classic same: hallway straight through from front to back door, chimneys inserted in the cross partitions between

10

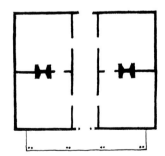

North Carolina Georgian-plan house type. Compare with Findlay & Co.'s square cottage plan (p. 124).

the side rooms. What emerges of particular interest, however, is that this single-storeyed plan type was regarded in later 19th-century America specifically as that of a "Southern" house, suited to a hot climate because of its corridor, which enabled easy cross-ventilation of rooms through the whole house. (Its "pyramidal" hipped roof was also seen as a Southern "folk" type, relatively rare elsewhere.)[3]

Deeper into the South, in North Louisiana, a similar plan type was common in Victorian times, but came from different origins. Its source was in folk dwellings of the basic two-roomed, rectangular type, adapted to the local climate about 1830. In this plan, known as the dogtrot, the two main rooms were separated centrally by a roofed and floored area about 8 ft. wide (2.5 m), open at both ends and thus forming a breezeway as well as an additional outdoor room. The dogtrot plan lasted a full century. A variant by 1840 enclosed the central area as a hallway, thus approximating the Carolina type described above but without the classical impulses. At length, from 1880, a further variant adopted the popular asymmetric, L-front plan with a projecting gabled wall adjoining a front veranda. The central broad hall remained, with doors at both ends, acting as breezeway and cross-ventilator. In this asymmetrical version, the resulting cottage was virtually identical in plan and appearance to the other most common New Zealand cottage type, the early gabled bay villa with its L-shaped front and shortened veranda.

Now these Southern house layouts were quite different from the typical American Victorian single-storeyed house of the Northern and Western states. There, in most if not all normal houses of one storey, the front entry was either directly into a main living room or into a separate "reception" vestibule, which gave only limited access to the parlour, and another general room (either sitting or dining) without hallway connection to the rest of the house. Frequently, five- and six-roomed plans were ingeniously designed to have no passageways at all. In characteristic American manner, a number of the social spaces were planned to interconnect; and main rooms, such as dining room and kitchen, were used normally for general circulation and access to bedrooms. This gregariously open plan enabled an even spread of warmth in the more severe winters of the Northern and Northwestern states. Also, in many cases, the house plan (and hence the lot frontage) could be narrower because of the absence of a longitudinal passage through the house.

This compact, interlocked type of plan was normal in California from the 1870s onwards for modest, single-storeyed farmhouses in the country, and for the "working man's cottages" as well as somewhat more extensive houses in the towns. In the narrower cottage types the entry porch or vestibule was usually set back alongside the gabled front parlour and abutting the dining room wall behind.

But the Southern house plan with its central hallway was also present, appearing as a country residence on California's coast and hot inner valleys. It must have been well established there by the 1870s: in the first year's issues of *California Architect and Building Review* in 1880, a succession of single-storeyed, central-corridor plans was published,

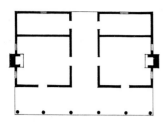

North Louisiana dogtrot plan, from 1830 onwards.

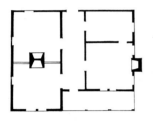

North Louisiana gable-front-and-wing plan, from 1880 onwards.

117a

116. *(opposite bottom) Narrow-plan cottages, West 19th Street at West Street, Oakland, California, c 1885– 1890. This normal US house plan (see* **117a***) has an entrance lobby only, opening to the Queen Anne gabled parlour (left) and the dining room projecting at the side.*

116

117b

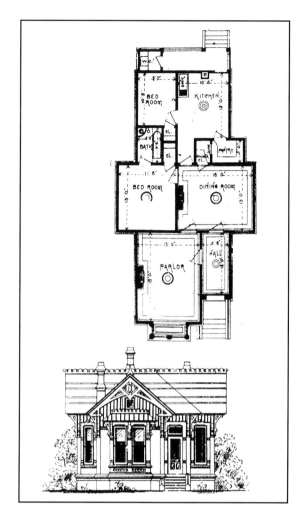

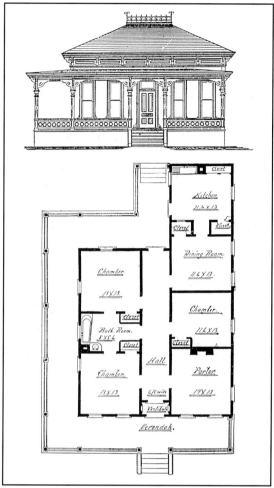

117a. *(above left) Typical American cottage plan without internal passage way, from* Quarterly Architectural Review, *April 1879, San Francisco. (The elevations show Stick–Eastlake-style features: see also* **122**.*)*

117b. *(above right) Country Residence, from* California Architect and Building Review, *May 1880. One of many designs from this date for houses with features very familiar to New Zealand: wraparound verandas, bracketed posts and upper eaves — and the central hallway plan.*

including the "straight-through" type, without specific comment on novelty or promotion of their planning. Indeed, plans of this type of "country" house made up a high proportion of all cottage plans published in the magazine's first few years. (Most appear to have been designed by the publishers, Wolfe & Son, as architects interpreting local norms.) Moreover, they often included shallow-roofed verandas across one or more faces, scroll brackets on chamfered, square wooden posts, splayed bay windows, eaves frieze and brackets — all by now familiar to us as the Californian style, and a foretaste of New Zealand's own later Victorian cottages, both symmetrical and with asymmetric projecting bay.

I have found no substantial precedent for this central-passage planning of one-storey cottages by searching American plan books from the 1840s to 1880, leading to the conclusion that the plan form may have been taken up in California in the knowledge of the Southern states' experience. Certainly, in national magazine articles and correspondence items, this plan type was often referred to as a "Southern" house, for warm climates. It had probably been popular for a decade or two in California since the gold rush ended, when the immigrants on the new frontier, settling in the hot central valley, had had to devise a suitable form for their new farmhouses out of their pooled experience and knowledge.[4]

In the January 1886 issue of *Scientific American (Architects and Builders' Edition)* from New York, an article on "Cheap Houses" referred to a central hallway plan, similar to both the New Zealand and North Louisiana gable-bay-and-wing types, as a "country dwelling" in which the hall provided "in summer a perfect system of ventilation". In their January 1889 issue a similar but larger plan was termed "a one-storey Southern house of low cost", having a hall 8 ft. wide (2.4 m): "The through hall we consider a vital necessity as it acts as a ventilating shaft for the entire dwelling." It is notable — bearing in mind the New Zealand inclination for single-storey living, as epitomised in our Victorian bay villas — that this horizontal type of layout was associated with California and its climate.[5]

It must have interested New Zealanders, extending their contact with California by the regular shipping of the 1870s, to discover such parallels in the nature of mutual house types, and to study their style directions. Our observers must have been impressed by the sophistication of popular

118

118. *(opposite) House, Islay Street, San Luis Obispo, California, c 1875–1880. Of single-storey "country-town" type with wide verandas, this early asymmetrical villa is handsomely proportioned, with simple Italianate brackets and trim.*

housing around San Francisco Bay and by the Americans' technical advances. The fact that our central hallway house plan coexisted there would have made it easy for our builders to adopt attractive "ideas from America" in the Californian style. This would have underlined our shared attitudes towards wooden houses and horizontal living in general. Equally, the lack of British precedents and guidelines in these matters would have played a part in our forebears' willingness to pursue a different lead.

Merchant suppliers and styles

PROGRESSIVE merchants of building supplies, with an ear to the ground and an eye to the market, had been attracted from the latter 1870s to certain American styles and developments which had promise for New **93** Zealand conditions and needs. As we have seen in the previous chapter, by the 1880s New Zealand timber merchants were offering a wide range of standardised components intended for embellishing external features on the common house. These ranged from prefabricated bay-window units some 9 ft. (2.75 m) wide in Italianate style, complete with moulded cornice, fretwork cresting, and all sashes (with, if required, panelled walls **fig. p. 114** below the sill), to a wide variety of shaped eaves brackets and fret-saw-cut gable ornaments. In aggregate, a large range of machine-made, mass- **fig. p. 103** produced woodwork items was available, all fully illustrated by line drawings in catalogues of patterns as presented by the merchants, and with close similarity to standard American products.

The range available here did not remain limited to Gothic and Italianate, but picked up shifts in style from overseas. In America, from around 1860, Davis and Downing's "wooden style" pioneering was carried further by others, into what was later called the Stick Style. European Picturesque style models of the early 19th century were being transformed into a strongly "timber-built" vernacular by plan-book architects such as G. Wheeler (English born and trained) and builder–authors including

119. *Atwood House, Hackensack, New Jersey, c 1876. A wholly American extravaganza, expressing the underlying bony nature of balloon-frame construction. The blend of wood-based styles earned the title of "Stick Style" many decades later.*

96
119 G. Woodward and, later, the Palliser brothers. Their designs expressed the thin, straight, sticklike nature of timber construction in certain features and proportions, which were applied to the basic Gothic and Italianate house forms: hard-angled and stiffly upright, square-sided bay windows appeared on simple boxy walls, often vertically boarded. Vincent Scully, the American historian who coined the name Stick Style, noted that the manner included elements of Swiss chalet, medieval half-timber and Japanese frame construction — "to enhance the expression of the skeleton frame". Writing in *The Architectural Review* of March 1954, he said that by the early 1870s "the articulated stick style clearly emerged at this period as the exuberant and expressive carrier of the American ver-

120, 121 nacular in wood". Many of its devices were used extensively on New Zealand houses through later decades.

The Stick Style became merged with the so-called Eastlake style, named after the English furniture designer C.L. Eastlake. His book *Hints on Household Taste,* published in 1868, was influential and popular in America, where it went through seven editions. It was a total manual of "good design" principles of convincing sanity, worthy of William Morris. Eastlake's book covered all aspects of interior furnishings, avoiding historical pretences and advocating a creative, craftlike attention to geometric patterns and shapings in wood that were "natural" to machine processes: repeated groovings, turned knobs, radiating patterns, drilled holes and the like. American builders adopted his interior-scaled "motifs" (but

122 not his lessons) and applied them in exaggerated forms to the exterior of houses, on gables, verandas and panels. Eastlake vehemently disowned all of this as an aberration; nevertheless, his style flourished as ornaments within the Stick Style manner, with much popular success. By the 1880s

123 this Stick–Eastlake style was taken up and widely applied in New Zealand, where its accessories continued to appear in catalogues well past the century's end (as they did also in America).

During the 1870s a new liberal style in red brick, called Queen Anne,

120. *House group, Tasman Street, Newtown, Wellington, c 1905. The practice of dividing walls into bold panels by a pattern of boards nailed over the weatherboarding is a common local application of the American Stick Style.*

121. *Edwardian house, Maida Vale Road, Wellington, c 1912. Stick Style devices are evident on this late Edwardian, in its batten-panelled gable and walls with scroll-bracketed frieze band. The English manner of the Domestic Revival shows in its restrained gable and one-way brackets.*

122. *Small villa, Los Angeles, c 1880. Combinations familiar in New Zealand of Victorian gables, bay windows and verandas on a prominent corner site, here ornamented in Stick–Eastlake style.*

was gaining definition in Britain. In the United States a blend of rich features from this and preceding Victorian styles was applied on a house body of strong and irregular volumes. These bolder forms were initially inspired by the virtuoso British architect Norman Shaw's "Old English" manner, displayed in his exciting and masterly country house designs of the late 1860s and 1870s, as an inventive reinterpretation of Elizabethan manors. The Americans developed their own style in wood, vigorous and assured, from his example. Their version was dominated by assertive gables on 40 to 45 degree slopes, often to the full width of the house front and with massive bargeboards. The domestic bay window with splayed sides was renewed from the Italianate, but was transformed by much broader proportions into a generous and calm form instead of the earlier constrained verticality. A move towards lower ceilings contributed to a horizontal emphasis. With a room-span bay window located beneath the front gable, either centrally or offset, the compound form possessed great expressive power. These strong elements dominated small, single storeyed "Queen Anne" cottages in the San Francisco Bay region in the 1890s, and were highly influential in the full development of the New Zealand bay villa.

124

Pl. 13

125

126
127

123. *Stick–Eastlake upper gable, Tinakori Road, Wellington, late 1890s. After 1870 a distinctive, popular styling feature of American houses was a twin window unified by an emphatic hood across it, seen here with elongated Eastlake brackets.*

124. *Grims Dyke (architect: Norman Shaw), Harrow, near London, 1872. Shaw's imaginative reworking of Old English gables and bay windows brought a vigorous response in America's development of Queen Anne style, with subsequent effect on New Zealand houses.*

125. *(opposite top) Cottage in Queen Anne style from* California Architect and Building News, *September 1894. The fully enriched American style for a small house. Innumerable New Zealand bay villas are of a remarkably similar appearance — and virtually identical in plan layout. (A raised basement is customary against local humidity.)*

126. *(opposite bottom) House in 6th Street, Berkeley, California, 1889. An unmistakable relative of the later New Zealand bay villa, this "workingman's cottage" is one of many in Queen Anne style surviving in the East Bay cities. (The balustrade and central steps have been altered.)*

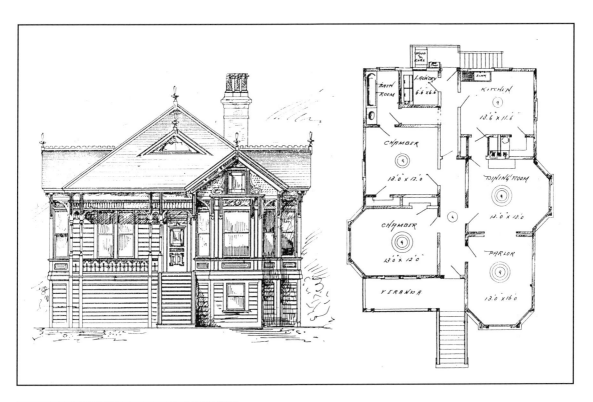

127. *Bay villas in Tole Street, Ponsonby, Auckland, c 1905. New Zealand progeny of the American Queen Anne-style cottage, in a typical street view which, nearly a century ago, could have been duplicated throughout this country.*

Bay villas and gabled bays

IN order to clarify some major aspects of the Victorian style at work, by studying a part representative of the whole, let us look at one of the most characteristic aspects of the external appearance of New Zealand villas: the design of those dominant, gabled wall faces. In discussing the evolution of folk forms out of the simple rectangular hut (see Chapter 1), I described a common modification made to the basic form by projecting asymmetrically one room and the roof over it, usually with a gabled end. Cottages of this type appeared occasionally from the 1840s in our early towns, such as Nelson and New Plymouth. This distinctive universal type is known commonly in the United States as an "upright-and-wing" or "gable-front-and-wing" house.

In an effective early development, the room was projected some 5 ft. (1.5 m) to meet the line of a veranda across the house front. The plan thus neatly dealt with two amplifications of the basic form, each in a due proportion: of the two front rooms, one was differentiated to be a more

83

Pl. 14

spacious living room or "parlour"; and the full-frontal veranda was reduced in length, although to a still adequate size.

The success of the format is proven by its persistence through the rest of the century and on into the 1910s. It was normal for the front gable and veranda to face the street in towns — or even a country road — regardless of orientation: social conformity was more valued than sunshine in "front of house". But the front "porch" in New Zealand towns does not seem to have reached the social importance it had in America for greeting neighbours as they passed by. Perhaps our restrained British ways prevailed. And British, too, was an attitude occasionally expressed that it was preferable to look out on a fully sunlit garden from a shady porch or room rather than to see only the shadowed back of the flowers. (This may well counter the popular rebuke that British emigrants built houses and schools "the wrong way round" in the southern hemisphere.)

A constant accompaniment of the Victorian gable was the bay window, either square-sided or with splayed sides as part of an octagon. Bay windows and the British have been inseparable for many centuries: there are beautiful examples from their medieval period, ranging from tiny oriels to vast, mullioned, glass walls of "solars" in the great houses; and classical houses were often graced by simple bays of rectangular or part-octagonal form. The Gothic Revival and Italianate styles ensured that the bay window continued into New Zealand's Victorian houses from the 1840s onwards, to culminate in the ebullient Queen Anne style at the century's end.

Pl. 15

The combination of ornate gable above bay window became a prime field for the expression of Victorian taste, reaching heights of ingenuity and using a fascinating variety of decorative devices. It is interesting to consider the lines of the development in New Zealand of the gable-bay system on our populist houses, as set out in the typical sequence illustrated in colour plates 18–21.

Pl. 18–21

It emerges from this that the key to understanding the main system is the frieze band. This acts as the controlling line which, with great simplicity, joins the complexities together in a clear relationship. It marks the virtual outline of the house for the builder's use in setting out all of the works (ignoring the standard splayed cut-offs at the bay corners). The focal corner brackets always lie in the line of this frieze. At the final stage the frieze band is suppressed; but by this time the builder's basic set-out comes as second nature.

From an analysis such as that illustrated in the plates one realises the rich potential in the standard New Zealand (and American) system of the Victorian and Edwardian gable-and-bay combination; and one appreciates the enormous range of design variations available. No such rationale was applied to gables and bays in 19th-century Britain. But here, the major parts of gable-and-bay as well as the decorative supporting members were open to a wide choice. An orderly basis of choice was governed by those timeless elements of geometric design — triangle, rectangle and octagon, combined in a classic architectural "pediment-on-entablature" relationship. The horizontal entablature had long been present as the

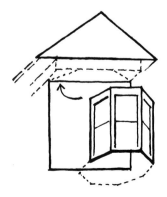

The gable-frieze-bay elements.

128. *Bay villa in Herne Bay Road, Auckland, c 1905. The classic* **128** *bay villa in New Zealand, fully developed with returned veranda, Eastlake-style brackets and gable peak ornament with massive finial, pendant and crosstie — completed with "eyebrows" against the sun. (Compare with* **126**.*)*

ubiquitous, deep, flat band up at the top of most walls, carrying solid brackets under the projecting eaves — a characteristic feature of New Zealand's wooden Italianate houses. The pediment, as always, was inherent in the triangle of the roof gable.

The main areas of design activity are at the corner zones under the outer points of the gable triangle: the enrichment around these areas is a game that is played out in complex variety. The everlasting versatility of this design method lies in the fact that the central zone between the corners is relatively neutral: the widths of flat surfaces, including the gable, and the number of windows, can differ to suit different room widths without affecting the crucial corner zones and their interlocked play in space.

Observe also the development from the first stage, in which the individual parts remain clearly self-contained and separately articulated as in classical methods of design, to the later stages, where many of the parts lose their independent identity, being merged into an all-inclusive yet complex overall form. A powerful, unifying design method is at work.

From system to style

THIS consistent *system* of interchangeable, highly designed elements, producing well-proportioned and unified designs, did not arise by chance — let alone in some colonial timber company's workshop or drawing office.

129. *Squared bay, Masons Avenue, Herne Bay, Auckland, c 1910. A late variant shows the flexibility of the theme. Elegant upright face brackets flank incredibly delicate gable brackets, of furniture scale. Pierced fans decorate veranda and gable apex.*

It belongs within a strong and inventive Victorian style, evolved from a long heritage. To be identifiable, a "style" must have certain characteristics: first, a constancy in basic forms; and second, a specific vocabulary covering related details and ornamentation. In the case of the gable-and-bay, a flexible but universal set of the same simple forms — triangle, rectangle and 3-dimensional part-octagon — became the basis for an infinite variety of ornamented parts, within the limits that constituted the *style*.

The gable-and-bay system relied on two distinct factors. First, the on-site construction of the basic "shell" framing was straightforward, despite the apparent complexity of final appearances. Its primary set-out and heights in relation to the rest of the house were virtually unchanging. Even the gable-end frame was readily supported by rough framing between the windows on the bay facets. Second, individual choice of ornamental details was vast, from a range of factory-produced components, most of them of wood, shaped into decorative, non-structural forms. "Cantilever" scrolled brackets were available in standardised dimensions for nailing under the projecting gable corners, profiled eaves brackets for the frieze band, crosstie and king-post finials in the gable apex. Further flourishes were often contributed by the builder in the way of scallop-edged bargeboards, curvaceous sill aprons, and sundry mouldings and panels.

129

The close study made above of the gable-and-bay combination — one of the major themes of the New Zealand Victorian villa — is intended to illuminate the Victorians' design approach to the popular house by spotlighting one of its most characteristic parts. Here, the part stands for the whole.

The term *kit set*, which has recently been applied to this kind of design, might be misinterpreted. It was not a case of purchasing a kit set of parts out of which a particular house form would arise, but rather of choosing a specific house plan and its general form, then making a

130
131

selection from interchangeable parts for its elaboration and ornamentation. The significant accomplishment had been, above all, that of arriving at unvarying, basic framing shells geared to receive any "bag of tricks" of premade components, selected at will from suppliers' catalogues.

The Victorian gable-and-bay, to which such components were attached, was no naive amateur concoction (although crude versions inevitably did occur); rather it was a powerful and recognisable set of forms and details working together in a systematic fashion. It was based on a sophisticated combination of constructional elements enriched by historical decorative forms, used in fresh ways in the manner of the Victorians. The elemental forms of gable and window bay provided a strong theme, capable of

Pl. 16

making the most of the play of volumes between the "solid" form of an angular bay and the consequent "voids" under the corners of a projecting gable above. The system was equally fruitful in the design of two-

Pl. 17

storeyed houses, where the bay was simply repeated vertically. Similar principles were applied to most aspects of house planning and design, based on variable combinations of standard "shell" elements, including rooms, hallways, verandas, etc., and their individual elaboration was chosen from the building merchants' catalogues of parts.

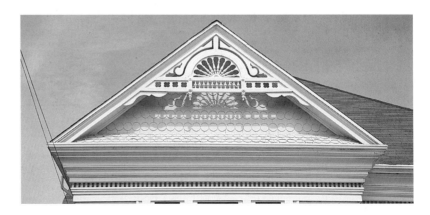

Victorian verandas

THE veranda appeared early in our story as a component of the New Zealand house plan. Up to 1840, in a variety of layouts, this multi-use combination of sheltering structure and "space in between" was detailed without affectation in the restrained Regency idiom. Simple, slender wooden posts, evenly spaced, carried a plain, light wooden beam at the roof edge of most mission and merchant houses, as a well-proportioned, purely structural, colonnade. In some cases trelliswork wholly filled occasional bays between columns, coolly screening the space behind (as at the Paihia Mission); in others, paired posts enclosed a lattice or tracery, resembling light pilasters. The simplest of arcs might link post tops to roof edge. **13**

12

46, 54

While veranda frames of folk houses continued unadorned for decades, other houses more conscious of the "picturesque" styles placed brackets at post tops, pierced with Gothic Revival three-leaf or geometric profiles, some as panels between twinned posts and others in long, flat, Tudor arch forms, as at Oneida and Te Makiri. More romantically "picturesque" was the use of forked tree branches as post and bracket, in England for "ornamented cottages" and locally on Colonel Wakefield's house of 1841 in Wellington. With the Italianate style came the heavily chamfered, 4 in. (100 mm) square, capped veranda post, most lasting of all our Victorian columns. Above the cap, Italianate brackets were at first only modified struts, with a curve or two added and perhaps an enclosed circle. The Italianate square column was rivalled only late in the century by the Eastlake style of turned column, with "table-leg" profiles of multiple grooves, recessed bands and rounded ends. **62, 60**

53

109

115

In the previous chapter I discussed at length the growth of the prodigious veranda-bracket family, aided by America's perfection of the scroll saw by midcentury. A vast range of designs was developed, from both Gothic and Classical style sources. Commonly, a shallow arc containing

132. *Cottage veranda, Elgin Street, Grey Lynn, Auckland, c 1890. Gothic-style detailing in "trefoil and dagger" brackets, forming a pointed arch between paired posts, and with quatrefoil running frieze: all standard New Zealand-catalogued ornamentation.*

132

100, 108

126, Pl. 20

98

Gothic cusped circle-and-leaf tracery curved up to merge into the underside of the roof fascia beam, with a turned acorn drop making an accent at the junction. The brackets were gradually deepened, their outline becoming more modelled and rhythmical, and the posts were often paired about 15 in. (380 mm) apart with special "Siamesed" infill tracery. The Italianate style soon took up the classical S-shaped scroll, on which endless ornate variations of brackets were produced in New Zealand, as we have already seen, as well as in America. For many designs, matching sets were available in two sizes: 2 ft. (600 mm) long for veranda brackets, and 3 ft. (900 mm) long for the projecting eaves brackets under gable corners above bay windows. (Interestingly, the equivalent brackets in America had the same dimensions.)

34

Earlier, from the 1850s, the lower edge of many veranda fascias was cut with scalloped patterns, similar to canvas awning fringes or valances on French and Swiss cottage eaves, and was often pierced to exploit the play of light and shadow on walls. These "curtain pieces" were echoed in the repeating shapes at the foot of canopy boards, widely used on railway buildings both in Britain and America as well as in New Zealand. A next step saw the popularity of pierced frieze boards, a fretwork chain of Gothic or Classical motifs contained within a long rectangular border about 9 in. deep (230 mm). Attributed to Japanese influence in 1880s America, where it was known as an "open-work fascia", the frieze was fixed below the roof fascia beam, thus deepening the proportion of the veranda roof with

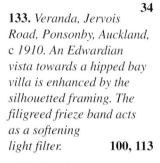

133. *Veranda, Jervois Road, Ponsonby, Auckland, c 1910. An Edwardian vista towards a hipped bay villa is enhanced by the silhouetted framing. The filigreed frieze band acts as a softening light filter.* **100, 113**

a lacy fringe. (The outlook, too, was improved from within the veranda and house, as the glare contrast between roof beam and sky was softened by the fringe as a delicate filter.) In Stick–Eastlake style, elongated "face brackets" with a prominent ribbed profile were often fixed on and above veranda posts, thus uniting veranda brackets and frieze. In this style and Queen Anne, turned spindles like tiny balusters, often with pronounced knobs, filled the frieze; and in Edwardian times after 1900, plain, spaced battens ended the series.

133

115

Apart from the early "colonial houses" with tentlike roofs overall, the Victorian veranda roof itself was always separated from the main roof, with its own slope and profiles, until the Edwardian period combined them again. It was covered virtually invariably with corrugated-iron sheeting on a shallow pitch, either straight, slightly concave or convex, or with a boldly rounded lower end (or "bull nose"). The curvature was done manually on roller jigs. If the dished, concave roof line arose from canvas

134. *Veranda, Dr Clarke Homestead, Whangarei, 1885. All main rooms have tall French doors onto this sparsely elegant country veranda. The graceful upper structure, with draped roofing iron, is the ultimate in economy of means.*

awnings in the Regency, the bull-nosed profile surely suggests the shape of Victorian umbrellas. This heavier form was part of a general enlargement of later houses, greater stud heights and a coarsening of proportions and details. Throughout the Victorian period, however, the veranda roof framing was always minimal and elegant, with slender rafters cut to the curve and at very wide intervals, and with a bearer cut in at midspan to support the roofing. All was smooth finished and painted: only in superior work was the ceiling boarded to conceal the corrugated iron.

Victorian and later Edwardian verandas in New Zealand fall into four main plan types. In two of them the verandas were attached to generally symmetrical house forms. The first lay fully across the main front of the house; the second extended across the front and down both sides. From early Victorian times, a third type was seen on the asymmetrical, L-shaped house front, where the veranda occupied three-fifths of the house width beside the projecting bay. In the fourth type, asymmetrical also, the veranda of the third type was extended down one side as well, usually to meet a matching bay projection. In the Edwardian decade this "corner villa" type managed a remarkable diagonal symmetry of its own through emphasis on the corner, often having a gable, an angled bay window, or even the front door and entry steps, on the corner diagonal axis. All four types of veranda planning were equally at home for two-storeyed houses, which simply repeated the single-storey layout to greater effect, on houses often enlarged to a grand scale.

The fourth type, the corner villa with its variations, also occurs in many forms across America and, on heavy brick villas, in parts of Australia as well. The later American Queen Anne house increased its sculptural modelling with a variety of turrets; and its hallmark, a rounded tower with conical roof, was often attached full height to a corner of the bulky house. Generously broad verandas often extended round the irregular profile of the house base.

A distinctive combination of veranda and doubled bay windows

134

108

17

135

Pl. 22

136

Pl. 24

137

135. *(opposite top) Bay villa with veranda, Ohinerau Street, Remuera, Auckland, c 1900. Shallow bull-nosed roofing on a late-Victorian veranda, with rich, surface-carved brackets and frieze, and face brackets above Eastlake-style posts — domestic in scale and reposeful.*

136. *(opposite bottom) Corner-angle bay villa, Clonbern Road, Remuera, Auckland, c 1910. Diagonal symmetry with angled entry steps and door under a pyramidal roof. The Stick Style veranda is unusually spikey, with turned and shaped brackets and frieze "knitted" together.*

137. *Corner-angle bay villa, Washington Street, Princeton, Kentucky, 1890s. An American example of diagonal symmetry in a villa. Its angled entry, flanked by gabled bays, has an interesting late-Eastlake scheme of ornaments. (See also* **115.**)

138. *Double-bay villa,
Wright Street,* **138**
*Newtown, c 1900.
The splay-ended recess
of the central veranda is
mated with the splayed
bays in a charming
combination, common in
Wellington and apparently
a uniquely New Zealand
creation.*

139. *(opposite) Veranda
porch, Masons Avenue,
Herne Bay, Auckland,
c 1910. Exuberant and
beautifully worked out,
this Eastlake-style porch
is raised above the veranda
roof to join the eaves line
of the house in a stylish
American manner.
(See also* **114.***)*

deserves mention, as a subgroup of the first type above. In a modest villa design popular in Wellington around the turn of the century, a small veranda lies between two normal splayed bay windows on the one-storey villa face. This open veranda shape, as an elongated hexagon, is related to the adjoining closed bays in a kind of positive-negative interlock. The splayed roof edge of the veranda repeats the splayed bay tops, unifying the house design by amplifying its rhythms. I am not aware of any common overseas equivalent to this effective design unit, which appears to be solely a New Zealand creation. Interesting variants on the theme occur, including generously scaled versions in the Wanganui district.

The Victorian system and popular culture

LATE Victorian house-design systems provided the builder with a working vernacular style, supported by basic plan guides and catalogues of standardised parts, which readily enabled him to produce sure solutions satisfying the tastes of would-be owners. An impressive range of well-tried decorative elements, consistent in style and scale, was available for the builder to use within an easily understood design system.

With the increasing use of applied ornamentation, patterns inspired from Gothic or Classical origins were mixed without a thought for

historical consistency. A shift had occurred world-wide towards more eclectic attitudes by which a designer felt free to choose any detail or style from any period which he considered suited his project. By century's end, the attention of house builders was centred on making the most of the invented ornamentation which fitted our popular villa forms, not on reproducing some known historical model or its parts.

By and large, the character of these New Zealand houses comes from a carefree and exuberant mixing of features fashionable at widely different times across 40 years or so. Although to many people the ornamentation may since have seemed misguided, the tastes of the period dubious and its excesses deplorable, there is a strong and distinctive flavour in the stylised character of the villa throughout New Zealand. In the total view, it is a rich display of popular culture at work — even if the designers of the kit set of parts seem to speak with an American accent.

This Victorian achievement is impressive in its strength of style: there is endless delight in the individual variety of gable bays and verandas along a street, yet they are sufficiently alike to stand together as a family **Pl. 23** — as a social group. The versatility and creativity of local New Zealand builders and designers is exhibited in the endless variations composed on the styles' main themes, in adapting stylised forms and system building into local, often unique, combinations. The infinite variety of subdivision widths in the larger cities, such as Wellington, spawned an enormous range of house types. The impression is gained that a catalogue of forms and types would show a considerably greater variety than would appear in a comparable Western American town's Victorian heritage. With much **138, 139** inventive talent and ingenuity, New Zealand builders created individual interpretations of broadly American-based styles, in handsome and original combinations of the style components.

How, one might well ask, did this sophistication of style and inventiveness in wood construction come about in an isolated country within a few decades of its founding? And, moreover, in one populated from a motherland with minimal current traditions of construction in wood? The proposition that the style and techniques were created by immigrants in this pioneering land, exploiting timber resources for the construction of ordinary houses and guided by the imitation of house forms and decorative devices known at "home", proves difficult to sustain. The architectural precedents found in British works in the Gothic Revival and Italianate styles were practically all carried out in masonry and stucco. No doubt some New Zealand resident craftsmen and architects could — and for public buildings often did — translate such forms into wood, as we have noted. But it is unlikely that builders of everyday houses throughout the country would have followed these few examples. More than this, the New Zealand house types are very different from any familiar British works: they do not *look* like the British houses of the time.

An alternative proposition, that our elaborated Victorian house types evolved independently out of the earlier colonial practices, and that all the later techniques and decorative forms were devised here, is equally difficult to sustain. Attractive as it might be as a cause for national pride, it presumes an unreal detachment from the rest of the world during half a century, and implies a phenomenal level of inventive design skill, beyond credibility for "a small community in a small country" (as Ngaio Marsh saw us).

The facts are that New Zealand was not detached from the world, let alone the Pacific; and that for many years prior to the decades in which our developed Victorian villas were being built, very similar designs, systems and types of wooden Victorian houses and ornamentation were built in the United States, on the West Coast and elsewhere. As we have already seen, numerous American architects and builders with their draftsmen had been redesigning wooden versions of English and European stone and brick styles during most of the century.

It is generally assumed in New Zealand that our Victorian house styles came to us directly from Victorian England. Yet you will seek in vain in British towns for normal, everyday houses of the common

142. *House in Hamilton Street, Herne Bay, c 1910. A two-storeyed house with verandas of generous scale, directly comparable with the previous illustration (**141**) in its twin-windowed bay face, shingled gable end and turned veranda columns.*

people that look like ours, for streets lined with freestanding, wooden, two-storeyed upright houses, or with single-storeyed Victorian villas centred in their own gardened plots. In England's crowded towns and cities they simply did not exist. But in the towns around San Francisco Bay, and in many other Californian and Western United States towns, you will find immediately recognisable wooden Victorian houses, standing freely in their own space, still lining street after street — and astonishingly familiar to New Zealand eyes.

  Writers dealing with the history of New Zealand's older houses have generally skirted the question of isolating a consistent pattern of influence from the United States on our commonest house types, in particular the Victorians. Beyond noting individual examples or occasional features that "appeared" somehow on houses here, from a known American style or practice in the latter 19th century, little attention has been given to gathering together the body of influence as a whole.

  Given the unlimited variety of design under Victorian methods it is all the more significant to find houses in New Zealand and the United States that are so closely alike in style when any combinations of the enormous Victorian vocabulary were possible. Moreover, design of the commonest houses in both countries was a virtually anonymous process occurring through the builders directly, who would tend to follow suit on stock solutions. Architects certainly played a part initially in designing basic elements and themes of this decorative vocabulary and publicising them in the United States. But with the development of mass-production technology and its related marketing practices, especially in America, Victorian house design became an early example of a machine age "builders' vernacular", of and for the common man.

  I recently invited a British-born couple, New Zealanders of today who had emigrated in 1950 in their twenties, to try to place a number of

140
141
142

Pl. 24 *(right) Clark homestead, Waipaoa, near Gisborne, c 1890. Enwrapped by grandly spacious two-storeyed verandas on three sides, this magnificent Italianate country house uses colonial elements to achieve a peak of comfortable wellbeing. (See also* **38 – 40**.*)*

Pl. 25 *(below) Bungalow in Lockett Street, Lower Hutt, c 1925. This exemplary redwood bungalow was imported precut from Seattle as a complete design, with American double-hung windows and frank carpentry details in struts and rafter ends. (The porch was originally open.)*

Pl. 26 *(top left) Bungalow in Maple Street, Rawlins, Wyoming. The essence of the American bungalow's character is seen at its simple best in this pleasant example, far from its Californian base.*

Pl. 27 *(left) Bungalow in Victoria Avenue, Remuera, Auckland, 1915. Built from the first with its full flourish of low-pitched gables, this partly two-storeyed bungalow is an early essay in the dynamic Californian style.*

Pl. 28 *(above) Bungalow in Tulloch Avenue, Wanganui, c 1920. A clear demonstration of the serene ease of expression attainable by a capable designer working within a New Zealand bungalow style. An indication of what could have been developed into a truly valid national form.*

Pl. 29 *(right) "Moderne" house in Marina Grove, Lower Hutt, 1940. The graphic qualities of this dramatic facade echo the promise of "the future", glamorised in the late 1930s by Hollywood and the exciting world fairs just before the Second World War.*

Pl. 30 *The Lawn, Boynton Road, Maidenhead, Berkshire, c 1905. This large Edwardian house in Britain typifies solid values of the English tradition, favoured by many New Zealand architects and their clients. Casement-windowed bays and clear-cut gables are set against high, tiled roofs.*

house photographs which I presented to them without identification. (They were, in fact, of several Californian wooden houses of the 1880s, which closely resembled some Wellington house types.) "One thing is sure, they're not from England!" was their opening remark. It was not only that they were of wood: the type of house was not familiar in the British context. They were freestanding family houses, on their own plots of land, individualistic, and bigger-scaled than the British norms. These one- and two-storeyed houses, though, were like everyday homes in the smaller New Zealand town, spread in low density on generous plots of land.

The people's house in Britain and New Zealand

WHERE the speculative houses in our antipodean country were mostly freestanding in form and individualist in aspect, their counterparts in Britain were generally the reverse. Since class came into every issue of housing in Britain, it is probably necessary for clarity to define the relevant New Zealand social group in English terms as ranging from middle working class to medium-towards-upper middle class. This group, in Victorian days in an English town, would have occupied attached row houses of   **63** which the basic form and plans remained largely unchanged through the second half of the 19th century. Their position on the class scale was indicated by a progression from the plainest of brick walls and windows on a minimal plan layout, through minor decoration added to doorway or window lintels and slightly larger rooms, into perhaps a boxed window and a moulded brick cornice line; thence to bay windows and larger rooms,   **143** elaborate moulded terracotta corbelling at the cornice, and raised gables with ornamental brick patterns. Firmly in the middle class by this latter   **70** type, such terraced houses were substantial and well built, with pleasant interior spaces.

143. *Terraced houses in York Avenue, Lincoln, Lincolnshire. Lower middle-class English houses of some substance, shown in fully detailed wooden bays and moulded terracotta corbel blocks at the eaves. The houses look small in scale and in overall height.*

Few tangible influences can be seen in New Zealand stemming from British terraced houses. Houses for the New Zealand man in the street were of a different nature from those provided for his equals in Britain. For example, English houses in general are noticeably smaller in scale than our typical Victorians, with storey heights 2 or 3 ft. (600 or 900 mm) lower than ours, and with their floors close to the ground and upper eaves close to window heads. Their overall height appears diminutive — as if three-quarters full size — to New Zealand eyes accustomed to our loose-limbed, two-storeyed Italianate houses and unconfined villas. British room sizes and window areas are also small by comparison.

Looking for fully detached Victorian houses of the common man in England as precedents for ours in New Zealand proves a vain exercise. There, such houses were normally those of the well-to-do, invariably of two or three storeys, and were of different character and materials from

144

144. *House in Franklin Road, Bournville, Birmingham, c 1895. An uncommon single house to compare with the common New Zealand two-storeyed villa. Brick, with Gothic-style stone details, timbered gable and wooden bay window — all of totally different expression from our local houses.*

our own. If there was any emulation of them in our common houses, then in general that came to us by the medium of American translations, as we have seen.

The difference in character is most marked between our Victorian villas and British terraced houses. In our lightly populated land and mild climate, our houses gained an easygoing spaciousness and connection to their sites that suited an outdoor-living people. Their prevailing wooden construction contributed the air of a lifestyle of apparent transience and flexibility, with a hint of the "tentlike" ideas underlying their origins in the Picturesque and Regency times. By century's end these houses shared an up-to-date style (including its American overtones) with a bright smartness — even some gaiety — in their individuality. Many of our forebears lived in streets of smiling villas, cheerful extroverts putting on their show.

In contrast, the equivalent dwellings in Britain were crowded together, sharing a restrained uniformity but preserving a private world within. Small in scale, as units of a tightly knit community, they speak of an urbanised, indoor-living people. The unvarying brick construction of monotonous long walls, with only minor variations of detail and few gardens, had a ponderous effect on the street: permanent, impersonal and aloof — even dour in aspect. The dwellings along the street were two dimensional, indeterminate, closed to view.

145. *Villa in Coates Street, Hamilton, c 1910. A most typical image of the New Zealand bay villa. Yet every attachment to the basic shell is American styled, from spindled grilles to toothed barge-boards, from finial base to veranda brackets. (The bracket design is No. 2028 in* Universal Design Book, *Chicago, 1904.)*

145

Chapter 9

Bungalows Reborn

Home in the suburbs

FROM pioneering days, many immigrants aimed for generous house sites. In rural areas they might thereby lift their condition to that of self-sufficient yeomen, while those in towns could readily achieve something akin to American ideals of the suburb. The die was cast early for large plots of land, and it persisted: the Kiwi's fixation on "the quarter-acre section" as his birthright and yeoman goal dominated other domestic land-use considerations far into the 20th century. The human price paid for this "freedom and privacy", however, was often isolation and suburban neurosis: the rich complexity of the life known in dense British towns, with their variety and sense of community, was not replaced by living in a Picturesque flower garden. And nationally the economic cost was high, in unduly stretched streets and service lines.

From 1901 the further extension of the tramways, now electrified, opened up new land areas close to cities for low-density subdivision, allowing the desirable convenience of single-storey living. In California likewise, around 1905, new freedoms through increased mobility and land expansion promised a more relaxed way of life which was embodied in a new popular house type, the informal, single-storey California bungalow.

Into the Edwardian decade

IT was well into the Edwardian decade, after the death of Queen Victoria in 1901, before New Zealand's late-Victorian houses reached their culmination, both in quantity and in style. In several respects their style was already out of date, at least in overseas terms. While England was revitalising vernacular forms in her refreshing Domestic Revival before 1900,

86

147. *(opposite) Corner-angle bay villa, Design No. 28 in* New Zealand Homes: Sixty Practical Designs *by J. Christie, Auckland, 1916. Still promoted at this late date, the eclectic design mixed features and stylised ornament from several decades.* **146**

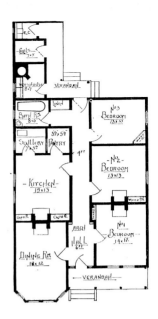

146. *Lodge at Shere Manor (architect: Edwin Lutyens), Surrey, 1894. Traditional English forms in stone, brick, roughcast and oak are here inventively combined in the fresh manner of the Domestic Revival.*

we were embracing American Queen Anne-style features — already out-moded in the US by 1895 — and were adding them to the prevailing Italianate forms on our villas. Time lags such as this appear to be due largely to reduced activity during our economic downturns (for example between 1880 and 1895).

As a result, New Zealand did not follow strictly a succession of dis-tinct styles in the order that they occurred in America. Instead, during the late-Victorian and Edwardian period, our builders merged and mixed those styles freely. A wide range of ornamental features was in use, some of which had appeared in catalogues as far back as 1880. The resulting com-binations were often adventurous, often quaintly charming, in their un-sophisticated freedom from stylistic rules. Indeed, the kaleidoscopic variety and vivacity of much of New Zealand's turn-of-the-century housing stock could well be seen to surpass the relatively conservative norms of their equivalents in the US.

127

147

*New Zealand bay-villa plan, from the same 1916 plan book as **147**. Compare with the US plan in **125**. By now the parlour had been replaced by the New Zealand "dining" room for family living.*

100

129

Pl. 15, Pl. 23

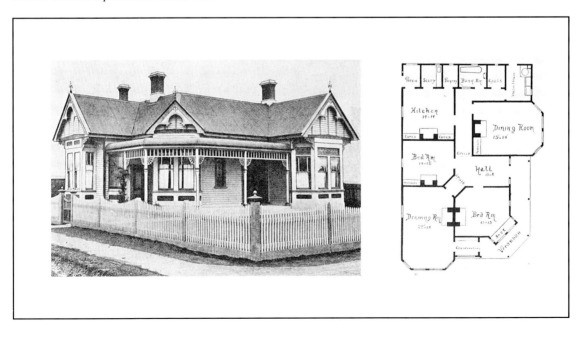

A degree of style selectivity did occur though, since several styles popular in America were virtually ignored here. These included the 1880s' highly characteristic, mansard-roofed Second Empire style (of cartoonist Addams macabre fame) and the two-storey, hipped-box, Colonial Revival house which supplanted Queen Anne US-wide by 1900. But the Californian bungalow we did not ignore.

The bungalow lineage

fig. p. 42

THE earliest antecedent of the bungalow, in the form of a Bengalese native house with verandas, has been touched upon in Chapter 5. During the past two centuries the word *bungalow* has been applied in England to the relatively uncommon single-storeyed house in general, sometimes with connotations of the Picturesque "ornamented cottage" in its gardened landscape, more often with recreated images of Indian Service days. Its line of descent was continuous through 50 years, from being a decorative whimsey of the landed gentry in the early 19th century (as we saw in Chapter 6), to being made liveable as an upper-class "country place", and, at length, to being simply a relaxing family retreat.

Living totally at ground level, close to Nature, was a novelty to the English, with their custom and status symbol of "sleeping on an upper floor", as Hugh Braun put it. Around 1870 a few brick "bungalows" were promoted near the coast at Birchington — low and rigidly straight, with end gable overhangs in Loudon's and Downing's "bracketed" Swiss cottage manner. The type had a vogue as seaside or — because of the absence of stairs — retirement houses. In due course, the eastern American states followed the English model with "cottages" on Cape Cod, and thence across the continent by the 1880s to the West.[1]

In California a local mix, blending Spanish hacienda types and Japanese roof forms with Arts and Crafts design and American Queen

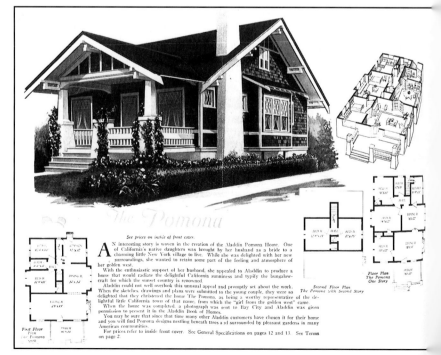

148. *Bungalow design from Aladdin Co. catalogue,* Aladdin Homes:"built in a day", *Michigan, 1919. "California bungalow" gables on emphatic brackets, and a deep porch with oversized, tapered supports. A true kit-set, low-cost home from the 1905 pioneers of mail-order precut houses.*

Anne cottage layouts, was developing before 1900 towards the characteristic California bungalow we know so well. The English Arts and Crafts
resistance to industrial production in the latter Victorian period inspired
an American following, led under the "Craftsman" title by Gustav Stickley
in New York from 1895. Their "homespun" handcraft contribution to the
American bungalow was given direction by Frank Lloyd Wright's new
organisation of domestic space, responding to social changes afoot, with
a new order of horizontal connectedness in low-scaled spaces and broader
proportions. All of these streams (and more) converged about 1900 in the
California bungalow, described by Stickley as "a house reduced to its
simplest form". David Gebhard, mindful of William Morris's unrealised
hopes, saw it as "the closest thing to a democratic art that has ever
been produced". From a generous porch one entered straight into the large
"family room", with no hallway — and no parlour: a new social order,
informal and non-historical, was shaping towards the liberated "flapper"
age. This development marked a break with decades of Victorian house-
building in the western United States.[2]

The bungalow type had, in fact, been introduced into New Zealand
just before 1900 by local architects, notably Goldsbro' and Hurst Seager,
returning from abroad with English Arts and Crafts ideas and aware of
the 1890s American Shingle style in large houses with wide, low-gabled
forms. A first major American-design bungalow — Los Angeles — was
built in Christchurch by 1913, combining both of these styles with
authority. After 1918, numerous "Californian" bungalows were imported
as precut redwood-framed kit sets from suppliers on the West Coast, including Seattle and Canada. They came complete with joinery, boarding
and even scaffolding, every part stencil-labelled. Full-blooded bungalows, they had all the Californian hallmarks: multiple gables over-
lapping at the front, gable at the side, overhanging eaves with exposed
rafters. Significantly, the age-old shallow veranda was changed to squarer
proportions, becoming an open-air room. But the popularisation of the
Californian bungalow style in New Zealand came mainly through syndi-
cated newspaper articles from America and "bungalow books" of designs
and plans, widely circulated and very influential on local builders' houses.[3]

149. *Bungalow in
El Molino Street,
Pasadena, Los Angeles.
This rakish example shows
a Japanese attitude in its
roof lines and heavy timber-
work, handled here in
"Craftsman" manner, on
boulder supports. The walls
are visually suppressed.*

148

149

Pl. 25

Pl. 26

150. *Bungalow in Gloucester Street, Wanganui, 1920s. Here is the classic bungalow expression, low-pitched and sharp-profiled. Penetrated by space, a light framework hovers over a massive base.*

Bungalow v villa

HOW radical this low-slung Californian bungalow must have appeared in the context of our Edwardian towns just before the 1914–1918 War. Its novel form soon overwhelmed the long-established Victorian house types from which it differed in almost every respect — in its scale, proportions, window shapes and types, roof forms, ceiling heights, plumbing, lack of ornaments, even its dark, natural colours. As might be expected, it was reviled initially by the establishment and English-oriented local architects, who saw this bungalow as an intrusion from the upstart Wild West. But its popular success was rapid, here as in California. At a time of so- **150** cial change, its frank use of simple materials and unaffected sheltering forms underlined a new freedom from convention among the common **151** people. An unsophisticated product, it spoke of cosy domesticity, of a popular culture, and of an Arts and Crafts pleasure in humble construction. Above all, the new bungalow form was eminently practical, a natural for our temperate climate, and an *artistic* house for the common man.

Many practical reasons assisted the change from villa to bungalow. Victorian high ceilings made heating difficult and were often dispro-

151. *Bungalow on corner site, Kensington Avenue, Petone, 1920s. An "everyday" house of unsophisticated grace, this side-entry New Zealand bungalow has Arts and Crafts details in its boxed windows, arched porch and bell-cast shingled aprons and gable.*

portionate in smaller rooms. Moreover, high walls were costlier, needing more materials inside and out. The casual style of the bungalow enabled living rooms to face the sun, not necessarily the street, and entrances to be at one side. There was a reaction against exterior ornament and mouldings that had lost their meaning for most people: the bungalow's restrained style and subdued detail marked a return to simplicity. Its internal planning was more informal and varied than the villa's standard central passage and string of rooms on each side. But the conventional American bungalow plan, with entry direct into the livingroom, did not win wide favour here: in most cases the plan retained hall and passageways, although rooms were often linked by double doors.

148

Bungalows were less pretentious than the villa, more homely with their low fireplace nooks, natural wood panelling, built-in cabinets, and dark-stained wood in archways, plate rails and trim. The "sun room" with folding windows confirmed new indoor-outdoor attitudes. What is more, the water closet could be incorporated within the house, now that towns had piped sewer drainage.

152

Emphasising the horizontal lines of the bungalow, rows of casements replaced the vertical proportions of the villa's double-hungs. Window areas were considerably reduced: to many people the large glass area of Victorian bay windows was excessive for sun or privacy, and in practice had been countered by three-quarter-drawn blinds. Double-hung sashes, when aged, rattled in the wind or jammed; or when sash cords broke were left inoperable. Side-hinged casements were easier to deal with. (America continued with sash windows well into the 1920s.) With English-type fanlights above the casements, showerproof ventilation was achieved along with the characteristic New Zealand "leadlight" — from diamond grid to flowing patterns in textured coloured glass.

153

152. *Sitting room with inglenook (architects: England Brothers), St Albans, Christchurch, c 1910. All the bungalow characteristics are here, in battened walls, boxed ceiling "beams", natural woods and snug alcove with its ceiling and walls fully panelled.*

153. *Bungalows in Formby Street, Pt Chevalier, Auckland, 1920s. A run of dual gables with a light touch in a bungalow suburb. Californian pergola porches join English casement-and-fanlight bays — bowed and square.*

154

155

Californian bungalows anglicised

TOWARDS the end of the Edwardian decade in New Zealand, a reaction to late-Victorian elaboration toned down the villa style. Main roof forms were simplified, often rising in the American manner to a high peak and continuing straight down over the veranda. Wall heights were reduced, gables lower pitched, ornament was cooled in keeping with Arts and Crafts precepts — truly "diminished" villas, preparing the way to the bungalow. A transitional form of house in New Zealand, around the time of the 1914–1918 War, combined the calmed peak-roofed villa and the informal bungalow with its English casement windows.

By the 1920s the bungalow had become the predominant new house

154. *Transitional villa in Arawa Road, Hataitai, Wellington, c 1910. A characterful translation of standard villa elements into Arts and Crafts style, with casement bay, boards cut to curves, elliptical arches, and balusters pierced with heart motifs.*

155. *Transitional villa in Hutt Road, Petone, c 1917. The corner-angle bay villa is transformed towards bungalow terms, with casements and leadlights in a splayed bay instead of double-hungs. A side porch replaces corner verandas: otherwise the floor plan is essentially as in* **147.**

type in New Zealand, continuing until the Depression stopped building activity. It had not been a case of one-sided American influence, however. "Anglicisation" of the American form, by features stemming from the English Domestic Revival and "garden city" model houses, led to local modifications — notably in casement window bays. In England the larger Edwardian house, descended from Norman Shaw's "Old English" forays, had adopted broad casement-windowed bays; and smaller houses also favoured the vernacular side-hinged casement window.

156

Pl. 30

124

Perhaps the most pervasive casement variant was the curved or multi-faceted bow window. The popularity of this device, attractive in itself, arose largely from architect Charles Voysey's reworking of old forms on new houses in Surrey in about 1895. Set under a plain triangular gable, the two-storeyed bow window was taken up by Britain's speculative builders and employed *ad nauseam*, on endless rows of brick semidetached houses

157

158

156. *Houses in Meadway, Hampstead Garden Suburb, London, c 1907. Parker & Unwin's layout grouped houses effectively along streets. Houses by architects such as Baillie Scott adopted casement windows and pleasantly simple forms, ultimately taken up in New Zealand bungalows.*

157. *Norney (architect: C.F.A. Voysey), near Shackleford, Surrey, 1897. Voysey's unconventional modelling of bold forms, with great simplicity, established new patterns which were spread throughout Britain in speculative housing estates.*

158. *(below) Semidetached housing estate, Harrow, London, c 1920s. One of the better-looking samples of Britain's mass-housing solution between the Wars. Voysey's gable over curved bay was reduced to the banal by interminable repetitions.*

built between the two World Wars. Our local bungalow builders adopted the casement bay — either curved, or boxed-out and flat — and made it a hallmark of the New Zealand bungalow. America, too, made occasional use of a flat version, from its own sources.

An unfulfilled potential

THE New Zealand bungalow manner, at its best, approached a genuine folk style suited to our national character: practical minded, informal and

159. *Bungalows in Daniell Street, Newtown, Wellington, late 1920s. Variations on the New Zealand bungalow theme. All have bell-cast gable ends on stub brackets, exposed rafter eaves and the distinctive bow window with planked hood.*

160. *Bungalow at 1st Avenue and Maple, San Diego, California, c 1920. Casements, fanlights and flat bays occur on some American bungalows, carried over from the Craftsman movement and here mixed with traces of Spanish Mission woodwork.*

161. *Bungalow in Ngaio Crescent, Lower Hutt, c 1930. The relaxed informality and comfortable air of this house epitomise the New Zealand bungalow. With side entry and sun porch, it displays many favoured details of the national house type.*

Pl. 27

162

relaxed, sensible in its use of obviously wooden forms, but also expressing a comfortable wellbeing in touch with natural surroundings — close to the Kiwi ideal.

Within the 1900s decade in California, when the recognisable forms of the bungalow were taking shape there, the outstanding architect brothers Greene and Greene in Los Angeles raised the humble type to the level of high architecture. In a series of extraordinarily creative and expressive houses — some elitist, some basic — they did much to

162. *David Gamble House
details (architects: Greene
and Greene), Orange
Grove Avenue, Pasadena,
Los Angeles, 1908.* **Pl. 28**
*Adventurous forms
and sensitive detailing,
by architects whose work
raised the qualities of the
humble bungalow to levels
of high style.*

catalyse the bungalow into its distinctive style in California with an
assured vocabulary of forms. It is regrettable our popular bungalow house
type in New Zealand was shunned by the architects of the time and
allowed to drift, thus depriving it of the design skills and imagination
which might likewise have developed its full potential here, into a convincing and generously warm local style.

Hollywood thirties

AFTER the mean Depression times lifted a little in the early 1930s,
a reaction in make-believe was hardly surprising. It took the form of
a short-lived decorative style known then as Jazz Modern, Spanish
Modern, or Moderne (and later loosely renamed Art Deco). Again largely
163   America-sourced, it revelled in unsophisticated parodies on the austere

163. *Streamline Moderne
house in H Street, Eureka,
North California, 1937.
All the signs of a defiantly
futuristic style are here:
"flat" roof, circles, flush
walls with rounded corners
and repeated horizontal
bands. Surprisingly, such
houses are now rare in
the US.*

functionalism of 1920s European architecture, combined with Hollywood fantasies and decorated by streamlined motifs and Californian Spanish trimmings.

The style was propagated by popular US books of house plans and designs which strongly influenced our local builders and public to pursue the vogue as a "modern" successor to the bungalow. Moreover, it differed from the cool restraint of the new state house. To most architects there was something "not quite proper" about this superficial fashion — at least **164** in its more exaggerated excursions. But its styling carried an exciting promise of the future and was popular on many houses in New Zealand up to 1940. Layouts differed little from those of conventional bungalows and two-storey houses, apart from the thrill of rounded corners and dramatic glazed staircases. The style was typified by a flat roof or, more **Pl. 29** commonly, a low-pitched slope concealed behind stepped parapets. It did not survive the Second World War.

Chapter 10

In English Style

The architects' houses

165. *Leslie Hills (architect: R.W. England), near Culverden, Canterbury, 1900. A new homestead on a great sheep run, retaining some English associations in its gables but displaying an eclectic range of American devices in its Stick Style tower and all-encircling, many-columned Queen Anne verandas.* **Pl. 30**

INDIVIDUAL architect-designed houses fall outside the main scope of this book; but interactions between populist house modes and architects' designs for the more affluent did occur which were of considerable significance. From early days in colonial New Zealand, architects were present whose work set standards of "correct" design in current styles; but throughout the 19th century their houses were a minuscule proportion of the total. Such house designs for the *un*common man — as single solutions to particular needs — had only limited influence on the "anonymous" houses built to meet the average man's needs.

As a rule, architects and clients for larger houses by the turn of the century favoured English traditional designs, where precedents suited. These often appealed to owners wishing to assert a family image of some English standing — whether actual or not. Most architects were British

166. *The Orchard (architect: C.F.A. Voysey), in Shire Lane, Chorleywood, Hertfordshire, 1900. Voysey's own house shows the essence of the English Free Style. His powerful simplifications, in strong gables and long bands of casements, were full of influence worldwide.*

trained (if not British born) and preferred the traditions they knew best. Working within the local practices of timber construction they generally elevated the detailing to a solid English manner more formal than American details (of which they were plainly aware). Merchants' town houses and run holders' homesteads usually adopted heavy Italianate or Tudor forms. Nevertheless, practical features of American style frequently appeared in their elaborated veranda-porches, extensive single-storey lay-outs and Stick Style square towers. Homesteads by R.W. England in the South Island and C.T. Natusch in the North, together with city houses by Thomas Turnbull (who had practised in San Francisco through the Italianate 1860s), F. De J. Clere and others, exemplify the hybrid image that resulted.

    Towards the end of the restless 19th century in England, the crafts-based rearguard action mounted since 1860 by William Morris and archi-

165

167. *Awatea (architect: R.K. Binney), in Bassett Road, Remuera, Auckland, 1922. Architects built many houses in English Free Style, marrying Voysey's simplicity to a warmth of materials and a joy of intersecting geometries in the Lutyens manner.*

168. *House in Seaview Road (architect: Gerald Jones), Remuera, Auckland, c 1920. Voysey's example in masonry freed the talents of several local architects towards creative work in the different discipline of wooden construction, as seen in this highly studied design.*

169. *House in Heriot Row (architect: Basil Hooper), Dunedin, c 1912. English traditions are here honoured with quality. Asymmetry with solid forms against double-veranda voids, and contrasts in colour and texture of materials, are sensitively balanced in Free Style.*

tect Philip Webb against machine-based production was at last winning ground. They had adopted the best qualities of rural English house traditions, in reaction to the excesses of Victorian design; and with other talented English architects and designers they had achieved a fresh handling of older forms, inspired particularly by the cottage vernaculars of

146
166
Sussex and the Cotswolds. Individual houses developed by the leaders George Devey, Norman Shaw, Edwin Lutyens, Charles Voysey and Baillie Scott placed England in the forefront of modern house design in Europe, with original images of calm domesticity, innovations in planning for comfort, and the rich textures and colour of local materials.

In the 1910s and 1920s most New Zealand architects favoured this now well-developed English mastery in domestic design, exemplified by Arts and Crafts, or Free Style, houses by late Victorian and Edwardian

156, 157
architects. The English style of this Domestic Revival was typified by a quiet strength and grace, high roofs and fine-lined gables, the avoidance of pretence and fussiness, with good craftsmanship and materials honestly used. New Zealand architects' English-style houses were of high

167, 168
quality in the work of R.K. Binney and Gerald Jones of Auckland, J. Chapman-Taylor and W. Gray Young of Wellington, S. Hurst Seager of

169
Christchurch and Basil Hooper of Dunedin. But their houses were a very small minority with little impact on the common man's house.

The American-style bungalow proliferated at builders' hands as

170. *Scott and Somerset houses, c 1920 and 1915, resited at Victoria University of Wellington. The peak of Edwardian composure (right) is contrasted with the agitated gabled roofs of a hybrid design* **170** *alongside, combining English boxed and oriel windows with bungalow carpentry details.*

the populist house of the time. Architects distanced themselves from it after their initial interest pre-War, and pursued the English Free Style almost exclusively. But some architects with ideals made efforts towards a national style to suit climate, materials and practical needs. F. de J. Clere, versatile Wellington architect of note, wrote in 1916 of the dilemma of "the copyist from English garden cities . . . to know how to introduce into his design a really useful veranda . . . a feature in general demand". But a merging of English and American styles was seen, particularly in larger Edwardian houses and in builders' designs, where bungaloid carpentry in walling details and exposed eaves rafters was combined with steep, English, asymmetrical gable roofs and Arts and Crafts boxed windows.[1]

By the 1910s, architects in England (led by Lutyens) were tempted back into the formal Georgian discipline: ultimately an enervating path which eclipsed Britain's ascendancy in domestic design for the next 20 years. New Zealand architects shifted similarly to Neo-Georgian a little later; but the pleasant English vernacular-based Free Style was continued by many into the 1930s. Some made a further swing, full circle, in the mid-1920s to the white, weatherboarded American Colonial style — a revival of the Virginian houses we have already met, in the mid-1700s in Williamsburg (see Chapter 4).

State houses

A most significant interaction between popular house forms and architects' designs, however, arose in the state housing policy adopted in 1936 by the first Labour government, after finding itself faced by a major housing shortage. A socialist ideal of quality for "the people's house" lay behind the choice of the traditional English cottage as the desirable model for a nationwide building programme. This political decision abruptly diverted the course of development away from the popular, low-pitched bungalow.

The Department of Housing Construction engaged local architects, through a competition, to produce the first range of house designs within the department's guidelines. These stipulated that the houses were to

171. *House in Lockett Street (architect: Bernard Johns), Lower Hutt, 1937. This modern version of English cottage style, at a larger scale, shows many of the style's pleasant features that were made standard in New Zealand state houses.*

Pl. 6
171

have a *dominant roof mass* and to be in the general style of the English cottage. This was no less than a version of the English Free Style in which local architects were already skilled; and, indeed, many of the designs adopted were of a high standard. But this policy, despite its worthy intentions, meant that the potential of the established bungalow was neglected, and this opportunity for design skills to develop it further as an indigenous New Zealand house type was lost.

172

Instead, the closed forms of the English cottage took its place, with small window areas, small cellular rooms off a narrow hallway, and no verandas or sitting porches — only minute recesses sheltering front and back doors — but with, on the other hand, a modern kitchen, built-in wardrobes and full services, all of high quality. The mould was set for the typical New Zealand house for decades to come.[2]

172. *An early state house of 1937 at Miramar, Wellington — and the bungalow form it supplanted. A paradox: Labour's "people's house" was given a sophisticated style in English tradition, replacing the bungalow, New Zealand's popular hybrid without pedigree, which already existed as an agreeable blend of British artlessness and Californian ease.*

British Airs and American Ways

> *We are hungry for the words that shall show us these islands and our-selves; that shall give us a home in thought.*

Robin Hyde

THROUGH our "readings" of the visible evidence of the buildings them-selves, typical and ordinary New Zealand houses and residential areas are seen to have been largely United States inspired, at least between the 1880s and 1930s. Yet this realisation runs counter to the commonly held assumption that (apart from bungalows) our houses were English-based in their forms and details. A confusing portrait of our forebears therefore emerges — facing two ways — which disturbs our customary image of unstinting devotion to Queen and Empire. It may be disconcerting to re-alise the extent of American formative influence throughout the very period in which sentiment for our British ties is commonly depicted to have been at a high level. Perhaps our forebears did not care to admit how much they owed to America. Or perhaps they simply took up the Ameri-can models that fitted their own pioneering outlooks and wishes, without thought of patriotism or paradox.

Making New Zealanders

BY the mid-1850s, little love seems to have been lost for England within the various groups of settlers. (Of the 32,000 total, only half came as Wakefield plan colonists.) After all, most of the emigrants had willingly left hardship or poverty in industrialised Britain. The settlers saw themselves as "British colonists" or "English subjects", but without limiting their hopes of bettering their position and chances in life.[1]

The new colony was, of course, expected to become a new "Britain beyond the Seas": the New Zealand Company's planned settlements were to mirror Britain's social structure, graded from privileged gentry to farm labourers. In the event, a shortage of resident landowners, and hence of agricultural work, first turned surplus labourers to other work in town, and then to become self-supporting on small land-holdings cleared from the forest. In this, as Rollo Arnold describes in *The Farthest Promised Land*, they realised their social ideal, that of liberated yeomen: a dream fed by awareness of the North American experience, where the independent yeoman farmer was hero of *the* myth of mid-19th-century America.[2]

At the opposite extreme, socially and materially, huge holdings of open land were occupied with little effort by a new type of colonial gentry, the "squatters", with money to buy flocks of sheep. The overly simple Wakefield plan had failed to work, and development became widely dispersed instead of concentrated as desired.

The other half of the country's settlements after 1840 occurred haphazardly from a host of beginnings, all similarly dispersed. Class divisions were not pursued, the freedom from fixed British ways was grasped, and settlers set about improving their lot through their own initiative. Innumerable letters "home" rejoice in better conditions than could have been hoped for in Britain; and a frontier-style life led towards a classless society, or at least one in which everyone acted as middle class. New Zealand's egalitarian and democratic attitudes were asserted, even presumptuously by some, from an early stage.

With economic troubles and Maori dissension increasing through three decades of colonial rule, there was widespread ill feeling towards a British Government reluctant to be involved in the needs of its unwanted dependent. An underlying urge to independent action was evident from the 1870s, when Vogel as premier demanded from Britain the right to enter trading agreements in wool with America (by the San Francisco route), and 20 years later when Ballance tried to have the powers of governors reduced. Keith Sinclair describes a growing sense of New Zealand nationalism among the common people in the 1880s and 1890s. He noted: "It grew up in defiance of the tradition among the better-educated section of the population that New Zealand was the 'Britain of the South'."[3]

In reality, by 1890 New Zealand was in a difficult state, facing disillusion at the unfulfilled hopes of the pioneers, unrelenting economic depression, misery among the poor, and lack of land available for small farmers. Political action was crucial to achieve a new economic and social order through regulation. The power of the ruling land-holding colonial gentry was broken by the Liberals' election to office in 1890. Enforced subdivision of large farm-holdings soon made land accessible to new settlers, and a more democratic representation was instituted, including votes for women. A radical path of social justice was taken, leading the world towards the welfare state. Modern New Zealand emerged as a changed society with a new confidence. "New Zealand is the birthplace of the Twentieth Century," wrote Professor Frank Parsons in his *Story of New Zealand*, published in Philadelphia in 1904. And strong US socialist policies (voiced by the Knights of Labour, centring on workers' rights) backed the legislation of Ballance's and Seddon's administrations through the 1890s.

By 1900 a lack of interest in Empire matters was evident. The *new* New Zealanders — local born, now outnumbering immigrants — had unqualified feelings for their native country. In historian W.P. Morrell's words, quoted by Keith Sinclair: " . . . they had as New Zealanders their own individuality, . . . they were not . . . merely Englishmen living over-seas". Given impulses to independent action even in the 1870s, now strengthened by a sense of nationality, it is likely that New Zealanders asserted their will by pursuing whatever solution appealed strongly for any matter in hand, regardless of allegiances to England.[4]

Not surprisingly they joined in the spirit of their Pacific regional context, where many solutions could be found in the enterprises of the Americans. From them came lessons arising from their wood-based building techniques, as well as their appealingly fresh Victorian house styles and open-spaced living patterns in towns. New Zealand life was coloured by an increasing American awareness and influence in day-to-day realities.

British airs

IT appears, then, that our late Victorians and Edwardians continued to refer to Britain as "home" and to render homage to "the dear old country" in sentiment and loyal support, while in many of the practicalities of life in this new land they marched to a different drum — that of our neigh-bours on the American West Coast. This influence appears strongly in many fields, particularly those involving popular tastes, technology and trade, and it reflects many parallels between our people's aspirations and America's achievements. Clearly, New Zealand found in the US attractive, ready-made answers to shared problems of inhabiting a new world and of making fresh starts, in the very times we are com-monly said to have been "more British than the British". An American bias was evidently moving deeper into our way of life; but a leavening of "British airs" was to remain as a restraining element of sensibility and informed taste, to temper the popular culture.

The two broad streams alluded to here within New Zealand society, which were seated not so much in class as in economic position, are revealed by our houses:

> *popular* tastes, shared among members of a community and
>   tending towards American fashions and ways; and
> *cultivated* tastes, individualist in nature, characteristic of
>   leaders in the community, and tending towards British airs
>   and traditions.

Both are parts of our social whole, our egalitarian New Zealand society. Interaction led to levelling (as in the case of state houses) rather than division into strata.

From late in the 19th century it was often said approvingly that New Zealand was "the most dutiful of Britain's daughters". In historian Keith Sinclair's view, our people's "reputation for a somewhat excessive devotion", beyond the normal bonds of sentiment, was not always justified. This has not deterred a succession of prime ministers from using such rhetoric as a political ploy, persuasive in negotiations with the British Government. Richard Seddon was the earliest, at the turn of the century, in his "clamorous patriotism" and noisy support for an imperial federation including colonial self-government — while shrewdly angling for a voice in British foreign policy.[5]

Motherland "apron-strings" rhetoric and jingoism are readily taken up in the press and are echoed in common talk, thus shaping attitudes in the public mind. But also, from the generation of my father (born 1895) my generation received a code of deep feeling, expressed in loyal phrases and references to "home" and "the old country". Perhaps this served to reconcile in some way the hurt felt in the disproportionate losses of our men in the Great War.

Granted, the feelings for "home" remained strong in many emigrant hearts in the 19th century. Sarah Courage put it clearly in 1896: "'Home' . . . always means England, for nobody except a born colonist calls New Zealand "home", not even those who, like ourselves, have been here over a quarter of a century."

The first issue of Wellington's *Evening Post,* on 8 February 1865, carried a small notice:

PRESENTS FOR HOME

W. JAMES, CABINET MAKER, Lambton Quay, will have a large assortment of articles in New Zealand woods in time for *Ballarat* and *Wild Duck.*

Ballarat and *Wild Duck* were ships then in port, bound for London.

In the 1940 centennial issue of *New Zealand from the Air,* Tasman Empire Airways advertised inauguration of the Auckland–Sydney flying-boat service: "The once remote Britain of the South is linked surely with its sister Dominion, and thence by Imperial Airways with the mother country." Blue Star Line offered accommodation on cargo ships: "It's a completely different way to travel Home." And up to the last quarter of the 20th century, the "home boats" took pride of place at their wharves in Auckland and Wellington.

The proud claim of our being "more British than the British" was heard well past the middle of the 20th century. On the other hand, many British emigrants in the second half of this century, on return to the UK after adopting New Zealand life for some decades, found they had become *less* British in their ways. Equally, many latter-generation New Zealanders, on answering the call to visit "home", were baffled at finding little in the UK that resembled their native land. On the other hand, if they passed through the US on their return journey, they had a foretaste there of New Zealand as a "little America".

This similarity was visible by the turn of the century. Professor Frank Parsons, again, said in 1904 of New Zealanders: "They are the Yankees of the South Pacific. In fact, New Zealand is a little America, a sort of

173, 174. *Main Street in Virginia City, Nevada (opposite), and the main street in Thames, New Zealand (below), together represent more than just their common backgrounds in silver and gold mining more than a century ago. Their present similarities indicate that the towns, as they have developed subsequently in*

173   *both countries,*

174   *continue to reflect likenesses in New Zealand and American cultures and ways of life.*

condensed United States." Another visitor, Mary Woolley from Chicago, wrote in *South Sea Letters* in 1906 that New Zealand was "far more like America than it is like Great Britain, but it is far 'slower' than America".

American ways

IN New Zealand's mood of the 1880s and 1890s, on one hand facing frustration and apparent failures and on the other boosted by a radical determination for change, the keen awareness of California's surging development must have been challenging. Here was a thriving new community, burgeoning from scratch on the Pacific coast in an isolation comparable to our own. Already their population was double ours. The urge to emulate and learn from their success must have been considerable in many fields.

New Zealanders no doubt took up American solutions simply because the model fitted their needs and wishes, without much thought of their "Americanisation". This term had been familiar since at least the 1850s, reflecting the potent character of that modern nation's fluid growth with, in those days, connotations of pioneering resourcefulness. Rather than impeding the growth of local ideas, this American awareness may in fact have stimulated our growing independence and sense of nationhood, impelling us towards efforts to walk on our own feet in the Pacific sector.

American styles adopted in New Zealand's popular housing from the 1870s to the 1920s may well have provided us with a symbol of the success this country sought — and at last achieved from about 1895 on. Trade also confirmed closer relations: the US received 1 per cent of our

175. *Kirkham Street, looking south from 10th Street, West Oakland, California, in 1940. Not only do the recognisable house types and styles evoke recollections of New Zealand streets 50 years ago, the very feeling of "ordinariness" is disconcertingly familiar as well.*

exports in 1870, 6 per cent in 1890, and a peak 16 per cent in 1920. Of our imports, 6 per cent were from the US in 1890, 18 per cent in 1920 and 1930.

No colonising theorist in Britain in the 1830s could have foreseen the opening-up of the American West Coast and its eventual effects on the developing Australasian colonies. A real and *modern* outlook emerged, not in the set and remote ways of Europe: the patterns of the 20th century were taking shape in a spirit of social freedom. With the entry of this new actor on the Pacific stage, and with its access to American thought as well as action, the expectation that New Zealand would become a replica of Britain in the South Seas was doomed. Direct links by sea travel ensured an alert and fraternal interest in our shared possibilities and problems. America was in the forefront of world inventiveness in applying power and technology to labour-saving equipment for farms, homes and offices, to machines for domestic tasks as well as in workplaces, and to new means of communication and entertainment. Here was the enticing promise of the "future". From the latter part of the 19th century, the model of the modern domestic world that New Zealand followed came more from the American West Coast than from Britain. The patterns of our own houses **175** and towns, the visible accompaniments to our way of life, became closely **176** akin to the American scene.

However, it was not only in building their homes that our forebears revealed their close interest in their dynamic neighbour. In small ways as well as large, they saw in the United States an alternative to Britain as a supplier of many of our developmental needs. I have previously referred to machines connected with the timber and woodworking industries, and to building techniques in general. American farm machinery was also widely imported: in the 1870s, under Premier Julius Vogel's initiative, large numbers of reapers and binders profitably worked wheatfields on the Canterbury plains, well into the 1880s.[6]

But it is the railways that offer the clearest indications of a willing alignment with American ways. In 1870 Vogel launched a bold immigration and public works plan to remedy the lack of a land transport system, which he believed was preventing the country's economic advance. The United States had just completed the transcontinental railroad through the West, and Vogel based his system on a similar

176. *Houses in Meridian Street, Elysian Park, Los Angeles. This ordinary street could as well be found in a suburb of Auckland or Wellington as in Los Angeles. The nondescript houses, only just bungalows, might be anywhere in New Zealand or the US — but not in the UK. "By their buildings ye shall know them."*

177. *A KA locomotive, New Zealand Government Railways, 1932–1950. Massive in aspect and festooned with exposed plumbing, the New Zealand-designed and built powerful K class has the character of great American steam locos on a smaller scale.*

economic plan for a light-freight, narrow-gauge railway. The American "revenue railroads" had opened up regions for settlement, initially on broad grants of land embracing the rail route which were sold after completion of the line. Vogel applied this principle to both rail and road proposals as security for an audacious 10 million pounds sterling loan over 10 years. From 1877 American locomotives were adopted, notably the fast and showy Rogers K class and the powerful Baldwins, giving the "American look" to New Zealand railways, which they have never lost. The US loco makers proved to be accommodating and became our major suppliers until the local production after 1900 of New Zealand designs, guided by US engineering. Not for us the sleek British engine, but the mus-

177 cular forms which culminated in our own great K class of the 1930s. Meanwhile, the Manawatu Railway Company was set up in 1881 by Wellington businessmen, who put virtually a complete US system into operation, with its locos, coaches with electric lighting, dining cars and colourful Americana. (It was bought by the government in 1908.)[7]

American style was extended to our wooden station buildings, especially those distinctive Edwardians designed by George Troup (as at New Plymouth, Petone and Foxton), with rusticated walls overlaid by an emphatic grid of dark boards, looking "half-timbered" but in full American Stick Style with added Queen Anne gable features. This long railways romance, fully in the public eye, may well have excited New Zealand tastes to receive other US offerings — including house styles.[8]

The present-day Mainstreet movement revitalising older parts of our towns is a current instance of New Zealanders adopting American ways that suit us. In fact it confirms a cultural continuity, since our towns' shopping streets typically follow the American pattern of wide and straight traffic routes, flanked by verandaed, flat-fronted buildings with parapets and loud signage.

A different kind of adoption was that at Brooklyn, the Wellington (not New York) suburb expanded by electric tramway in 1906, where the

178. *Chautauqua Industrial Art Desk, 1923 model scroll-easel desk with art slate, made by Myerson Co., Indiana. The "endless" scroll revealed topics such as simple accountancy, American birds in colour, laws of perspective — and here, aptly, a California bungalow with its plan.*

streets were named after US presidents. Wellington's tramways, indeed, started out with American-built cars in 1878, steam-drawn and replete with red velvet upholstery; and Dunedin's cable car from 1883 had New York-built cars.

Other instances of our looking to the United States, in addition to Britain, for the latest or the best answer to some development could readily be cited. In many cases a positive preference or enthusiasm for American style and products was evident, for the "American way" does generate enthusiasms, with a certain zest and unique flair. Popular in appeal and unsophisticated though it may at times be, it conveys an openness and vitality that are engaging.

I have often reflected on my childhood spent around the Hutt Valley through the 1930s — a typical enough childhood for a third-generation New Zealander, I should think. Yet I am aware of a strong American undercurrent, the extent of which surprises me: bedtime readings from Longfellow's *Hiawatha* at an early age, Tom Sawyer role models later, games of cowboys and Indians, Pontiac and Chevrolet family cars, California Syrup of Figs of dire recall. Soon came the revelations of a Chautauqua "home teacher" scroll-easel desk, years of stimulus from *Life*   **178** and *Saturday Evening Post* magazines, the exciting personality of late 1930s cars from General Motors, hillbilly songs — and so it went on. Even our family house was more American in character than I then knew.   **155**

In retrospect, I realise that it was through my father's open-minded interests that I was introduced to these things. Yet I always regarded him (as I am sure he regarded himself) as a typical and patriotic New Zealander. I do not recall either of my lively-minded parents as being unusually America inclined. Just fairly typical New Zealanders . . . But, I wonder, how much of American flavour lies within the typical New Zealander's make-up?

Although our country's main base stands on British customs and social institutions, our man-made surroundings — the towns and the houses we live in — owe much to American sources and stimulus. We should look, and look again, in order to see as if for the first time those things that have become too familiar to be noticed.

Notes

To ease reading of the main text, notes for sources and additional information are indicated at the end of a paragraph or group of paragraphs. References are listed in the same order as in the text. Page numbers are not always given if a work has an index.

Chapter 1 — pages 4–9

1. The width is limited by a capability to span the room safely with a manageable structure. Angles of roof slopes vary in response to local materials and conditions of rain, snow and wind; but a higher roof angle may also make further rooms possible within.

2. Batsford and Fry, *The English Cottage*, p. 17; Mellaart, *Earliest Civilisations of the Near East*, pp. 39, 81; Coblence, *Les Premières Cités*, p. 11.

3. Lloyd, *A History of the English House*, pp. 2–7; Batsford and Fry, op. cit.

4. Polack, *Manners and Customs of the New Zealanders*. Marsh Arabs living on the Euphrates Delta still build high-arched houses in the ancient manner shown.

5. Possibly stylistic precedents existed in the projecting of a central pedimented bay on Georgian mansions, or of a gabled dormer wall on Cotswold Gothic cottages.

Chapter 2 — pages 10–23

1. Fleetloads of a thousand or so deportees were landed, years apart, and virtually abandoned by an indifferent Colonial Office. The 11 ships of the first fleet in 1788 provided 16 ships' carpenters while they were at the colony, and a further 12 carpenters and one bricklayer were found among the prisoners (see S. Sidney, *The Three Colonies of Australia*). With good clay unearthed, brick-making kilns were active within a year. Timber from nearby forests was pit-sawn into framing or planks, and shingles were split for roofing to supplement the use of thatching or bark.

2. Bunning, *Homes in the Sun*; Rienits, *Pictorial History of Australia*.

3. Elder (ed.), *Letters and Journals of Samuel Marsden*, p. 231.

4. During his four-year wait in Sydney, Hall gained a working knowledge of colonial carpentry and of frame-and-board construction, seldom seen in his native Lake District.

5. Between 1815 and 1830, among the missionaries were at least three carpenters, three ironsmiths, a shoe maker and twine spinner, a school teacher and a farmer, as well as several clergymen. The building team was augmented by trained Maori sawyers and carpenters.

6. Elder, op. cit., pp. 497, 481.

7. Elder, op. cit., p. 395.

8. Elder (ed.), *Marsden's Lieutenants*, p. 243. Construction was by carpenters Fairburn and Bean, with major contributions by Butler and his son and by Maori sawyers. (Hall generally managed to find his services needed elsewhere.)

9. Both types are seen in early New South Wales. There, too, they were infused with a Late Georgian lightness gained in the passage of exotic ideas through England and between colonies (see Chapter 5). Fairburn and Puckey, stationed at Paihia, presumably built the houses.

10. McLintock (ed.), *An Encyclopaedia of New Zealand*, for Clarke; Elder, *Letters and Journals*, op. cit., p. 494, for Darwin.

11. McLintock, op. cit., for kauri gum and Clendon; Porter (ed.), *Historic Buildings of New Zealand, North Island*, for Clendon.

12. Elder, op. cit., Porter, op. cit. and McLintock, op. cit., for Busby.

13. McLintock, op. cit.; Knox (ed.), *New Zealand's Heritage*, sundry entries.

Chapter 3 — pages 24–30

1. Richards, "The Functional Tradition", *Architectural Review* 726 (July 1957, London), p. 28.

2. Jordan, *The English House*, fig. 38; Nairn and Pevsner, *The Buildings of England: Surrey*, p. 82; Batsford and Fry, *The English Cottage*, p. 83

3. Cook, *The English House Through Seven Centuries*, pp. 148, 229; Lloyd, *A History of the English House*, p. 142; Batsford and Fry, op. cit., p. 82, figs 109–13. See also Jordan, op. cit., fig. 209.

4. Newman and Pevsner, *The Buildings of England: West Kent*; Holme, *Old English Country Cottages*, p. 165; Batsford and Fry, op. cit., pp. 45, 48.

Chapter 4 — pages 31–9

1. Kimball and Edgell, *A History of Architecture*, pp. 532–4; Morrison, *Early American Architecture*, pp. 30, 138.

2. Morrison, op. cit., pp. 10, 31; Kelly, *Early Domestic Architecture of Connecticut*; Lloyd, *A History of the English House*, pp. 73, 76, figs 324, 673.

3. Interestingly, Virginians distinguished between the old *split* clapboards and the wider *sawn* weatherboards which, from their later introduction, were called 'weatherboards' by them — and still are (Morrison, op. cit., p. 138). Brunskill, *Illustrated Handbook of Vernacular Architecture*, p. 64.

4. Whiffen, *The Eighteenth Century Houses of Williamsburg*, p. 4; Morrison, op. cit., p. 33.

5. Quoted in Pevsner, *An Outline of European Architecture*, p. 710.

6. See Cook, *The English House Through Seven*

Centuries, and Batsford and Fry, *The English Cottage*, for sundry references.

7. Whiffen, op. cit., p. 99.

8. In *Small Houses of the Late Georgian Period* (1919), on Georgian houses in late 18th-century England, S.C. Ramsey commented on their similarity to contemporary houses in America and raised the likelihood of cross-influence from American Colonial houses. He writes: "We know that communication with the colonies was regular . . . and that during this time there was a constant interchange of architectural ideas . . . It is almost inconceivable that the distinctive work of the developed Georgian in America should have been without any influence on the designs of the English architects."

9. Ironically, popularity of weatherboarding in England was boosted by a stiff tax on the use of bricks, imposed in 1784 to offset costs of opposing Americans in their War of Independence and remaining current until 1850. Lloyd, op. cit., p. 142.

10. Whiffen, op. cit., pp. 99, 109. Diagonal boarding on dormer cheeks was common also in Savannah, Georgia, in the latter 1700s — not only flush-beaded as at Williamsburg but also 'saw-toothed', as standard in New Zealand. Savannah was a major seaport on the whalers' and traders' route between New England and the Pacific.

11. A ship's carpenter named Wise — of unrecorded nationality — was engaged from the start on the Mangungu mission house by the Reverend John Hobbs, himself an apprenticed carpenter. (I am indebted to Patricia Adams' research in this matter.)

Chapter 5 *pages 40–48*

1. Prefabrication of wooden houses, for example, was a long-standing practice. Preassembled house frames (no doubt in heavy tenon-jointed units) were shipped from New England to settlers in the West Indies as early as 1650 (Watts, *The West Indies*).

2. Morrison, *Early American Architecture*, pp. 135, 171. I am indebted to Dr Jessie Poesch for bringing the New York Cottage to my attention: see her "A British Officer and His 'New York' Cottage", *American Art Journal*, vol. xx, no. 4 (1988).

3. Pilcher, *The Regency Style, 1800–1830*, p. 69.

4. Reception porticoes, screened from the private dwelling spaces, were common throughout the traditional Islamic world. Portuguese explorers appear to have used their word *vara* (of Latin origin relating to "forked sticks", which was applied to grilles of balustrades, railings, etc.) to refer to the latticework on the Arab porches, seen in their early contacts. From the word for the part, it seems, came the word *varanda* for the whole.

5. Morrison, op. cit., p. 258; Noble, *Wood, Brick and Stone*, fig. 9-9; Kennedy, *Architecture, Men, Women and Money*, p. 68, and *Orders from France*, pp. 199, 201.

6. Fleming, Honour, Pevsner, *Penguin Dictionary of Architecture*, p. 22, Australia.

7. *Oxford English Dictionary*, 2nd edn; Morrison, op. cit., p. 357, and pp. 449, 490–510 for Harrison.

8. Cook, *English House Through Seven Centuries*, p. 229.

Chapter 6 *pages 49–77*

1. See Stacpoole, *Colonial Architecture in New Zealand*, p. 25 et seq.

2. Perhaps as seen in the 1846 edition of Loudon's *Encyclopaedia of Cottage [etc.] Architecture*. The house was based on a full mock-up, erected in England before emigration.

3. Clark, *Civilisation*, p. 169 et seq., 291.

4. According to Joshua Reynolds' *Discourses*, the Picturesque style sought an association of ideas affecting the imagination, such as the delight given by veneration for antiquity and ancient customs. To him, additions to old houses could make for irregularity so that they "acquire something of scenery".

5. Repton, *Fragments on the Theory and Practice of Landscape Gardening* (1816). Repton justified his use of apparently old-fashioned formal elements in his "natural" landscape designs by stating that "a Garden is a Work of Art using the Materials of Nature". Formal flower gardens did not exclude landscape but were woven into it. Pilcher, *The Regency Style, 1800–1830*, p. 41 et seq.

6. Andrew Jackson Downing's principal books are *Cottage Residences* (1842) and *The Architecture of Country Houses* (1850): see Clark, *The American Family Home, 1800–1960*, pp. 16–23 et seq., and Kostof, *America by Design*, pp. 21–8 et seq. For Davis see Kastner, "Alexander Jackson Davis", in *Notable American Architects* (J. Thorndike, ed.), p. 69 et seq.

7. For Highwic analysis see Anne Neale, "The Origins of Highwic", *NZ Historic Places* 39 (Dec. 1992), p. 4. For Te Makiri see R. Sales, "Early New Zealand Settler Cottages, 1850–70", University of Auckland B. Arch. thesis, 1970. In addition, evidence of American models for Te Makiri (such as Davis's Cottage Lawn) is now proposed. The general design and proportions are closely comparable, as also is the front gable (here boxed forward without relation to interior spaces, seemingly to repeat its model) as well as the configuration of the front veranda, main eaves fretwork, "gothic" gable window, chimneys and planform.

8. For Oneida (Wanganui) see Porter (ed.), *Historic Buildings of New Zealand, North Island*.

9. *Encyclopaedia Britannica*, 14th edn, vol. 17, p. 705, for Penn; Hayden, *Redesigning the American Dream*, p. 19–23, for Jefferson, Downing, Beecher.

10. Marshall and Willox, *The Victorian House*, general refs.

11. For ownership data see Clark, op. cit., p. 94, Marshall and Willox, op.cit., *NZ Official Yearbook, 1990*, p. 513, and Brookfield, *Historical NZ Yearbook*, p. 109. Comparable recent NZ figures are 68% from 1971

census and 75% from 1990 census.

12. For flower garden research see J. Harris, *Apollo* 380 (Oct. 1993, London), p. 227.

13. Dickinson and Gardiner, "St. John's Wood", *Architectural Review* 630 (June 1949, London), p. 273 et seq.; Summerson, *Georgian London*, p. 158–9.

14. Marshall and Willox, op. cit.; Jordan, *The English House*, pp. 111–13. Furneaux Jordan states (p. 113): "The spec builder and the landlord had had things their own way throughout the century. A series of minimum by-laws had dealt inadequately with safety and sewage. Beyond that neither decency nor amenity were thought of."

15. Pevsner, *Outline of European Architecture*, p. 557; Gloag, *Men and Buildings*, p. 168.

Chapter 7   *pages 78–120*

1. *Encyclopaedia Britannica, 14th edn*, for California history; McLintock (ed.), *An Encyclopaedia of New Zealand*, sundry entries; Turnbull, *The Changing Land*, p. 51.

2. Thomas Macky wrote home: "California will be a great benefit to New Zealand in giving it a good market for our produce . . . They do not grow anything there . . . There is no comfort there of any kind." He sold 5 tons of onions for 60 cents per lb.: in New Zealand they had cost 2 cents per lb. A 500-ton barque was bought from profits and used in the next two years for trading, in association with Robert Graham, with high returns. Late in 1850 Macky reported: "When I left, the population of San Francisco and the town up the river, and the mines, was fully 300,000. There are 700 ships laying in the Harbour, and every day the arrivals are from 5 to 50." I am indebted to Pat McCay for her permission to quote from letters in *Macky Family in New Zealand 1845–1969* (in-family publication).

3. Cowell Hall of California History, The Oakland Museum, Oakland, California.

4. Aidala, *The Great Houses of San Francisco*; Gebhard, *Architecture in California, 1868–1968*.

5. Turner, *The Frontier in American History; Encyclopaedia Britannica, 14th edn*, vol. 1, p. 769 et seq.

6. "Frontier values" are well illustrated by Wyoming, organised as a territory in 1868 to protect settlements along the Union Pacific railway. At its first legislature in 1869, women were given the right to vote in all elections — the first in the world. On the state's entry into the Union in 1890 an "equal suffrage" clause confirmed their right in the new Constitution. In another world's first, women served on a jury in Laramie in 1870.

7. Stoehr, *Bonanza Victoriana: Architecture and Society in Colorado Mining Towns*.

8. McLintock (ed.), *A Descriptive Atlas of New Zealand*, p. 69.

9. Guthrie and Larnach's enterprising "Dunedin Timber Yards & Steam Saw Mills . . . and Furniture Factories", in its 1874 "List of Prices" for local and imported products, announced: "We are importing direct from Great Britain, America, and other parts of the world, every article necessary for . . . our extensive business." American items listed included Clear Pine lumber [at twice the price of kauri T & G flooring], Oregon beams and planks, kegs of Cut Nails, and casks of Plaster of Paris. "Ornamental Brackets" and "Sofa Scrolls" in wood were also listed (without mention of source). E. W. Mills & Co. advertised in *Wise's 1883–84 Directory*: "Importers of every description of English and American Hardware".

10. The N.Z. Insurance Co. had already opened a branch in 1875; and this further investment in San Francisco property by the "progressive and youngest of Britain's daughters" was welcomed by the journal. The proposed building (in a surprising Moorish style with a Gothic spire) was also to house agencies of the N.Z. Loan & Mercantile Co. and N.Z. Stud & Pedigree Co., and the Bank of New Zealand's correspondent. (The 1906 earthquake and fire was a heavy setback but the insurance company paid out fully its $2 million losses, against liabilities covered of $3 million.)

11. For example, Swainn (ed.), "North Carolina Folk Housing", *Carolina Dwelling*, p. 40.

12. Wilson, *A Living Legacy: Historic Architecture of the East Bay*; Richey, *The Ultimate Victorians of the Continental Side of San Francisco Bay*. New Zealand taupata flourishes in hedges as "mirror leaf"; and tall Australian bluegum trees, grown from nuts sent back by a travelling Methodist bishop about 1860, still shed strips of bark on Alameda County — adding to our feeling of being among "Pacific neighbours". Our familiar radiata pine is native to the Monterey peninsula, together with macrocarpa (cypress): both were introduced to New Zealand from California.

13. Clere, "Domestic Architecture in New Zealand", *The Studio Yearbook of Decorative Art, 1916*, London, p. 122.

Chapter 8   *pages 121–57*

1. Early town development had very few planning controls: wooden houses were frequently built close to their side boundaries, but not touching, and the front wall was on the boundary. Side walls, often of two storeys and a mere foot or two apart, were protected against fire by corrugated iron sheets (under a Wellington bylaw from 1878), applied to opposing wall frames before being tilted up.

2. Wood, *Victorian New Zealanders*, 1974, p. 43 et seq.

3. McAlester, *Field Guide to American Houses*, p. 309.

4. In *Carpentry and Building* of March 1895 (New York), a letter from a Virginia builder illustrated a typical "Southern" cottage plan (similar to one in *California Architect* of May 1880), commenting: "Houses with connection from front to rear seem to suit better in this section [of the country] than those arranged in such a way that it is necessary to pass through one or more rooms . . ." Also, a letter was quoted in 1893 from "Tradesman" of Tennessee criticising architects' model house plans in which "the same design and arrangement

suitable for the bleak climate of the Lake region is equally recommended for the central South . . . Our Southern ancestors builded very wisely [*sic*], with an eye single to the requirements of the climate in reference to comfort and health." He cited homes with "broad shady porches, wide halls and commodious rooms, insuring the fullest ventilation by day during the hot season".

5. In May and August 1891, *Carpentry and Building* (New York) illustrated two houses recently built in southern California: of the first Californian Cottage, the paper stated: "The rooms are arranged upon one floor, this being the common practice in that section [Orange County] for moderate cost dwellings, as it is in the other sections of the country where the climate the year round is somewhat tropical in its character." Of the second, with a floor plan virtually identical to that of countless New Zealand villas, the article stated: "The house is typical of the moderate cost dwellings in that section of the country . . . Entrance to the main hall, which extends nearly the length of the house, is made from a broad veranda, the latter being an ever-present feature of dwellings in that locality".

Chapter 9   *pages 158–69*

1. Winter, *The California Bungalow*; Braun, *Elements of English Architecture*, p. 118.

2. Stickley, *Craftsman Homes*, p. 89; Gebhard and Winter, *Guide to Architecture in Los Angeles and Southern California*.

3. Ashford, *The Bungalow in New Zealand*, for Goldsbro' and Hurst Seager.

Chapter 10   *pages 170–74*

1. Clere, "Domestic Architecture in New Zealand", *The Studio Yearbook of Decorative Art, 1916*.

2. The Housing Department's standardised construction practices, utilising New Zealand-made materials, determined the economic bases, stock materials and methods of the house-building industry thereafter: concrete roofing tiles and precast piles, terrazzo sink benches, standard window joinery sections and profiles for all interior trim. During 42 years from 1937 the state built just over 100,000 houses — nearly 9 per cent of all New Zealand's houses.

Chapter 11   *pages 175–83*

1. Sinclair, *A History of New Zealand*, p. 98 et seq.

2. Arnold, *The Farthest Promised Land*, p. 260 et seq.

3. Sinclair, op. cit., p. 227.

4. Ibid., p. 232.

5. Ibid., p. 213 et seq., p. 223 et seq.

6. McLintock (ed.), *An Encyclopaedia of New Zealand*, vol. 1, p. 628.

7. Palmer, *Cavalcade of N.Z. Locomotives*, pp. 45, 52 et seq., 87; Stewart, *When Steam was King*, pp. 25–36; Troup (ed.), *The Steel Roads of N.Z.*

8. Staffan, "Railway Station Buildings", *NZIA Journal*, March 1965, pp. 43–70. Additional to this, it is of interest that the house of T. Ronayne, General Manager of Railways — designed by F. de J. Clere in 1896 at 50 Tinakori Road, Wellington — is in American Stick Style similar to that adopted for station buildings in G. Troup's term as "designing engineer" (architect) from 1902.

Illustrations Credits

The colour plates and all other photographs and line drawings, except those acknowledged below, were taken or drawn for this book by the author.

Archival photographs and prints, plans, elevations and catalogue pages are reproduced by courtesy of the sources listed alphabetically below.

Numbered illustrations

Alexander Turnbull Library, Wellington: **5** (F150857), **7** (18581/21032), **14** (F53312), **16** (F29695), **53** (F2441), **54** (51372), **65** (19106, Robin White Coll.), **67**, **81** (F152774), **83** (G5855, James McAllister Coll.), **86** (G22732, S.C. Smith Coll.), **107** (C16544, S.C. Smith Coll.), **111** (G10476, Steffano Webb Coll.), **112** (18580, S. Head Coll.), **152** (11079, S. Head Coll.); Athenaeum of Philadelphia, Pa.: **98**; Auckland Art Gallery collection: **17** (presented by Sir Cecil Leys, 1935); Auckland Museum: **4**, **12** (C19, 508), **46** (C189), **100** (C18,133); The Bancroft Library, University of California, Berkeley, Cal.: **104**; Chris Cochran: **103**; *Dover* Publications Inc., New York: **119** (from Gillon, E.V., *Early Illustrations and Views of American Architecture*); Los Angeles Public Library, Cal., Security Pacific Collection: **80**, **82**, **122**; Oakland Public Library, Cal., Oakland History Room: **85**, **175**; Otago Settlers Museum, Dunedin: **30** (William Meluish photograph), **110**; Dr Jessie Poesch: **35**; University of Auckland, Architecture, Property & Planning Library: **60** (R. Sales thesis), **147**; The Winterthur Library, Wilmington, Del., Printed Book and Periodical Collection: **148**.

Unnumbered illustrations

Alexander Turnbull Library, Wellington: **p. 14** (F156179)], **p. 22** (F29695), **p. 124** (137526); The Bancroft Library, Berkeley, Cal.: **p. 90**, **p. 116**; Dover Publications Inc., New York: **p. 82**, from Gillon, E.V., *Early Illustrations and Views of American Architecture*; Otago Settlers Museum, Dunedin: **p. 103**; University of Auckland, Architecture, Property & Planning Library: **p. 112**; **p. 114**; The Winterthur Library, Printed Book and Periodical Collection: **p. 106** (top), **p. 106** (bottom).

Other reproductions, in order of appearance, are gratefully acknowledged to the following organisations, individuals and publications:

8: Ford, C.B. (ed.), *The Legacy of England*, London 1935; **9**: Marsden, J.B., *Life and Labours of Samuel Marsden*; **18**: *Architectural Review* 726 (July 1957, London), (E. de Mare photograph); **25**: F. Cousins photograph, Essex Institute; **26**: Lloyd, N., *History of the English House*; **27**: Kocher and Dearstyne, *Colonial Williamsburg: Its Buildings and Gardens*, Williamsburg 1949; **p. 42** (lower): Lancaster, C., *The American Bungalow*, New York; **p. 43**: drawing by author from photograph in Morrison, H., *Early American Architecture*; **38**: W. Bartel photograph, in *Historic Sydney*, Dept. of Tourism, Sydney, 1978; **39**: Sherlock, P.M., *West Indies*, New York 1966; **40**: *Architectural Review* 606 (June 1947, London), (C.J. Laughlin photograph); **41**: *Architectural Review* 593 (May 1946, London); **50**: Goodhart-Rendel, H.S., *English Architecture Since the Regency*, London 1953; **59**: Madison County Historical Society, Oneida, N.Y.; **p. 131**: Swainn, D. (ed.), *Carolina Dwelling*, NCSU 1978; **178**: exhibit at Dawson County Historical Museum, Lexington, Neb., 1994.

Selected Bibliography

The following works were found of interest and helpful in the writing of this book, and are listed to assist a wider reading in specific subjects.

New Zealand and Australia

Apperly, R., Irving, R., and Reynolds, P., *Identifying Australian Architecture*, Sydney 1989
Arnold, R., *The Farthest Promised Land*, Wellington 1981
Ashford, J., *The Bungalow in New Zealand*, Auckland 1994
Bunning, W., *Homes in the Sun*, Sydney 1945
Christie, J., *New Zealand Homes: Sixty Practical Designs*, Auckland 1916
Cochran, C., *Restoring a New Zealand House*, Wellington 1980
Elder, J.R. (ed.), *Letters and Journals of Samuel Marsden*, Dunedin 1932
—, *Marsden's Lieutenants*, Dunedin 1934
Fearnley, C., *Colonial Style: Pioneer Buildings of New Zealand*, Auckland 1986
—, *Vintage Wellington*, Dunedin 1970
Hill, M., *Restoring with Style: Preserving the Character of New Zealand Houses*, Wellington 1985
Hodgson, T., *Looking at the Architecture of New Zealand*, Wellington 1990
Keith, H. (ed.), and Main, W., *New Zealand Yesterdays*, Sydney 1984
Knox, R. (ed.), *New Zealand's Heritage*, Wellington 1971–1974
McCormick, E.H. (ed.), *Making New Zealand*, Wellington 1940
McLintock, A.H. (ed.), *An Encyclopaedia of New Zealand*, Wellington 1966
—, *A Descriptive Atlas of New Zealand*, Wellington 1959
Main, W., *Wellington Through a Victorian Lens*, Wellington 1972
Munz, P. (ed.), *The Feel of Truth: Essays in N.Z. and Pacific History*, Wellington 1969
Oliver, W.H., *The Story of New Zealand*, London 1960
Palmer, A.N., *Cavalcade of N.Z. Locomotives*, Wellington 1965
Polack, J.S., *Manners and Customs of the New Zealanders*, London 1840
Porter, F. (ed.), *Historic Buildings of New Zealand: North Island*, Auckland 1979; ditto: *South Island*, Auckland 1983
Rienits, R. and T., *A Pictorial History of Australia*, London 1959
Salmond, J., *Old New Zealand Houses, 1800–1940*, Auckland 1986
Scott, D., *Inheritors of a Dream: A Pictorial History of New Zealand*, Auckland 1962
Shaw, P., *New Zealand Architecture*, Auckland 1991
Sinclair, K., *A History of New Zealand*, London 1959, 1980
Stacpoole, J., *Colonial Architecture in New Zealand*, Wellington 1976
Stewart, D., *The New Zealand Villa*, Auckland 1992
Stewart, W.W., *When Steam Was King*, Wellington 1970
Troup, G.F. (ed.), *The Steel Roads of New Zealand*, Wellington 1973
Turnbull, M., *The Changing Land*, London 1960
Wood, J. A., *Victorian New Zealanders*, Wellington 1974

Great Britain

Allsopp, B., and Clark, U., *English Architecture*, Stocksfield, Northumberland, 1979
Batsford, H., and Fry, C., *The English Cottage*, London 1938
Braun, H., *Elements of English Architecture*, Newton Abbot 1973
Brooks, S.H., *Designs for Cottage and Villa Architecture*, London 1839
Brunskill, R.W., *Illustrated Handbook of Vernacular Architecture*, London 1971
Cave, L.F., *The Smaller English House*, London 1981
Cook, O., *The English House Through Seven Centuries*, London 1968
Dixon, R., and Muthesius, S., *Victorian Architecture*, London 1978
Dutton, R., *The Victorian Home*, London 1954
Eastlake, C.L., *Hints on Household Taste*, London, from 1868
Fletcher, Banister F. and H.P., *The English Home*, London 1910
Gloag, J., *Men and Buildings*, London 1950
Goodhart-Rendel, H.S., *English Architecture Since the Regency*, London 1953
Gray, E., *The British House: A Concise Architectural History*, London 1994
Holme, C. (ed.), *Old English Country Cottages*, London 1906
Jordan, R. Furneaux, *The English House*, London 1959
Lloyd, N., *A History of the English House*, London 1931
Long, H.C., *The Edwardian House*, Manchester 1993
Loudon, J.C., *Encyclopaedia of Cottage, Farm and Villa Architecture and Furniture*, London, from 1833
Marshall, J., and Willox, I., *The Victorian House*, London 1986
Nairn, I., and Pevsner, N., *The Buildings of England: Surrey*, London 1971
Newman, J., and Pevsner, N., *The Buildings of England: West Kent*, London 1969
Papworth, J.B., *Rural Residences: Designs for Cottages, etc.*, London 1818
Pilcher, D., *The Regency Style, 1800–1830*, London 1947
Ramsey, S.C., *Small Houses of the Late Georgian Period*, London 1923
Service, A., *Edwardian Architecture*, London 1977
Sparrow, W.S. (ed.), *The Modern Home*, London 1906
Summerson, J., *Georgian London*, London 1945
—, The London Suburban Villa 1850–80, *Architectural Review* 620 (August 1948, London)

United States of America

Aidala, T., and Curt, B., *The Great Houses of San Francisco*, New York 1974
Baer, M., Pomada, E., and Larsen, M., *Painted Ladies: San Francisco's Resplendent Victorians*, New York 1978
Barber, G.F., & Co., *New Model Dwellings*, Knoxville, Tennessee, *c* 1895
Bicknell, A.J., *Detail, Cottage & Constructive Architecture*, Troy, New York, 1873
—, *Cottage and Villa Architecture*, Troy, New York, 1878
Clark, C.E., *The American Family Home, 1800–1960*, Chapel Hill 1986
Downing, A.J., *Cottage Residences*, New York, from 1842
—, The Architecture of Country Houses, New York, from 1850
Gebhard, D., *Architecture in California, 1868–1968*, Santa Barbara 1968
— and Winter, R., *Guide to Architecture in Los Angeles and Southern California*, Santa Barbara 1977
Handlin, D., *The American Home: Architecture and Society, 1815–1915*, Boston 1979
Hayden, D., *Redesigning the American Dream*, New York 1984
Hitchcock, H.-R., *American Architectural Books* (bibliography), New York 1976

Hobbs, I., & Sons, *Villas, Cottages and Other Edifices*, Philadelphia 1873

Hussey, E.C., *National Cottage Architecture*, New York 1874

Kelly, J.F., *The Early Domestic Architecture of Connecticut*, New Haven 1924

Kennedy, R.G., *Architecture, Men, Women and Money*, New York 1985

—, *Orders from France*, New York 1989.

Kostof, S., *America By Design*, New York 1987

Maas, J., *The Gingerbread Age*, New York 1957

McAlester, V. and L., *Field Guide to American Houses*, New York 1984

McMurry, S. A., *Families and Farmhouses in 19th Century America*, New York 1988

Morrison, H., *Early American Architecture*, New York 1952

Noble, A. G., *Wood, Brick and Stone*, Amherst, Massachusetts, 1984

Palliser, G., *Model Homes for the People*, Bridgeport, Connecticut, from 1876

Palliser, Palliser & Co., *New Cottage Homes and Details*, New York 1887

Richey, E., *The Ultimate Victorians of . . . San Francisco Bay*, Berkeley 1970

Shoppell, R.W., *Modern Houses; Beautiful Homes*, Co-operative Building Plan Association, New York, from 1887

Sloan, S., *The Model Architect: Cottages, Villas, Suburban Residences*, Philadelphia 1852

—, *City and Suburban Architecture*, Philadelphia 1859

Stickley, G., *Craftsman Homes*, New York 1909

Stoehr, C.E., *Bonanza Victoriana: . . . Colorado Mining Towns*, Albuquerque *c* 1975

Swainn, D. (ed.), *Carolina Dwelling*, North Carolina State University 1978

Thorndike, J. (ed.), *Notable American Architects*, New York 1981

Turner, F. J., *The Frontier in American History*, New York 1947

University of S.W. Louisiana, *Folk and Styled Architecture in N. Louisiana*, Lafayette 1989

Vaux, C., *Villas and Cottages*, New York 1857

Wheeler, G., *Homes for the People in Suburb and Country*, New York 1855

Whiffen, M., *The Eighteenth Century Houses of Williamsburg*, Williamsburg 1960

Wilson, M., *A Living Legacy: Historic Architecture of the East Bay*, San Francisco 1987

Winter, R., *The California Bungalow*, Los Angeles 1980

Woodward, G.E., *Woodward's Country Homes*, New York 1865

—, *Woodward's Architecture, Landscape Gardening and Rural Art*, New York 1867

—, *Woodward's National Architect*, New York, from 1868

General

Clark, K., *Civilisation*, London 1969

Coblence, J.-M., *Les Premières Cités*, Paris 1985

Fleming, J., Honour, H., and Pevsner, N., *Penguin Dictionary of Architecture*, London 1980

Gardiner, S., *Evolution of the House*, London 1975

Hitchcock, H.-R., *Architecture: Nineteenth and Twentieth Centuries*, London 1977

Jones, O., *The Grammar of Ornament*, London 1856

Kimball, F., and Edgell, G.H., *A History of Architecture*, New York 1918

King, A.D., *The Bungalow: The Production of a Global Culture*, London 1984

Mellaart, J., *Earliest Civilisations of the Near East*, London 1965

Pevsner, N., *An Outline of European Architecture*, London 1960

Pugin, A.W.N., *The True Principles of Christian or Pointed Architecture*, 1841

—, A.C.P., *Examples of Gothic Architecture* (3 vols.), London 1831

Rapoport, A.-*House, Form and Culture,* Englewood Cliffs, New Jersey 1969

Watts, D., *The West Indies*, Cambridge 1987

Index

Bold figures refer to illustration numbers, not pages. (Illustration references in the text are indicated in the text margin.)

Colour plate locations

Allen, G.F 63, **62**
American colonial houses 33, 35, 92, 131, 173, **25**, **27**
American influence in NZ 3, 20, 22, 175–7, 179–83
  on house design 9, 37, 39, 62, 90–94, 100, 104–8, 116–17, 152–4, 159, 161–4, 169, 180–82, **58**, **74**, **87**, **120**, **123**, **140**, **145**
  on popular culture 152, 181, 183
  on technology 181
  on towns 181, **173–6**; **Pl. 11**
  on transport 181–3, **177**
  architects' v populist design 170–74
  English tradition v American style 170–73, 177
Ashworth, Edward **16**, **17**
Auckland (1843) 22, 78, **17**
Australia 11–15, 102, **9**, **38**

Baillie Scott, M.H. 172, **156**
bargeboards 103–4(+**fig.**), **57**, **66**
Battle of the Styles 75–7
bay villa
  in NZ 101, 124–9, 140–44, **79**, **100**, **127–8**, **135**, **145**; **Pls. 15**, **18–23**
  in US 101, 137, **93**, **122**, **125–6**, **137**
  v corner bay 149; **Pl. 22**
  v corner-angle bay **136–7**, **147**, **155**
  v double bay 101, **92**, **94**, **138**

floor plans 159(**fig.**), **110**, **125**, **147**
parts catalogues 109–12(+**fig.**), 114(+**fig.**), **100**
Bell (Cpt M. Smith) House **24**
Binney, R.K. 172, **167**
Birmingham, housing **70**
brackets 83, 109(+**fig.**)–13, 115–17(+**figs.**), **98–104**,
  eaves 143, **89**, **104**
  gable 143, **103**, **100**, 125–9; Pls. 15, 19–21
  veranda 112(**fig.**), 122, 145–7, **78**, **82–3**, **100**, **103**, **113–14**, **132–8**, **145**
Brees, S.C. 52, **53**
brick, use of 5, 11, 14, 102
Brighton Pavilion (J. Nash) **51**
Britain
  classes 69–70, 72–3, 155, **70**, **143**
  NZ attitudes to 50–53, 120, 175–9
  NZ political stance 176–8
  wooden constructions 24
bungalow 42, 160–68 *passim*, **67**, **148–53**, **159–61**; **Pls. 25–8**
  "anglicised" b. 164–6
  California b. 160–66, **148–9**, **160**, **162–3**, **178**
  Indian b. 42(+**fig.**)
  NZ potential 166–8, 173–4
Busby, James (Residency) 19, 38, **15**, **31–2**
Butler, Rev. John 14–16, **10**

California **77**
  early history 78–81
  NZ parallels 86–8, 91–4
  NZ traders (1850s) 79–80
    prefab. houses to C. 80
  bungalow 158, 160–62, 167
Caribbean *see* West Indies
carpenters, early 11, 13–15, 21
  ships' 19, 21, 26, 30, 39
cast iron 102
catalogues, trade 106(**fig.**), 108–17 *passim*, 112(**fig.**), 114(**fig.**), 116(**figs.**), 135, **98**, **103**, **104**, **110**
Chapman-Taylor, J.W. 172
clapboards 32(+**fig.**)

190